D0764540

Becoming Functional

Joshua Backfield

SANTA CLARA PUBLIC LIBRARY
2635 Homestead Road
Santa Clara, CA 95051

Beijing · Cambridge · Farnham · Köln · Sebastopol · Tokyo

Becoming Functional

by Joshua Backfield

Copyright © 2014 Joshua Backfield. All rights reserved.

Printed in the United States of America.

Published by O'Reilly Media, Inc., 1005 Gravenstein Highway North, Sebastopol, CA 95472.

O'Reilly books may be purchased for educational, business, or sales promotional use. Online editions are also available for most titles (*http://my.safaribooksonline.com*). For more information, contact our corporate/institutional sales department: 800-998-9938 or *corporate@oreilly.com*.

Editors: Meghan Blanchette and Brian Anderson	**Indexer:** Ellen Troutman
Production Editor: Kristen Brown	**Cover Designer:** Karen Montgomery
Copyeditor: Rachel Monaghan	**Interior Designer:** David Futato
Proofreader: Becca Freed	**Illustrator:** Rebecca Demarest

July 2014:   First Edition

Revision History for the First Edition:

2014-06-30:   First release

See *http://oreilly.com/catalog/errata.csp?isbn=9781449368173* for release details.

Nutshell Handbook, the Nutshell Handbook logo, and the O'Reilly logo are registered trademarks of O'Reilly Media, Inc. *Becoming Functional*, the image of a sheldrake duck, and related trade dress are trademarks of O'Reilly Media, Inc.

Many of the designations used by manufacturers and sellers to distinguish their products are claimed as trademarks. Where those designations appear in this book, and O'Reilly Media, Inc., was aware of a trademark claim, the designations have been printed in caps or initial caps.

While every precaution has been taken in the preparation of this book, the publisher and author assume no responsibility for errors or omissions, or for damages resulting from the use of the information contained herein.

ISBN: 978-1-449-36817-3

[LSI]

Table of Contents

Preface

Although not a new concept, functional programming has started to take a larger hold in the programming community. Features such as immutable variables and pure functions have proven helpful when we have to debug code, and higher-order functions make it possible for us to extract the inner workings of functions and write less code over time. All of this leads to more expressive code.

Who Is This Book For?

I wrote this book for anyone who is interested in functional programming or is looking to transition from an imperative style to a functional one. If you've been programming in an imperative or object-oriented style, my hope is that you'll be able to pick up this book and start learning how to code in a functional one instead.

This book will teach you how to recognize patterns in an imperative style and then walk you through how to transition into a more functional one. We will approach this by looking at a fictional company called XXY and look at their legacy code. We'll then refactor its legacy code from an imperative style into a functional one.

We're going to use a few different languages throughout this book:

Java

    I assume that you are familiar with the Java syntax. The version used in this book is 1.7.0.

Groovy

    Using this language, we can keep most of our existing Java syntax; this helps us begin our transition into a fully functional language. I'll explain the main parts of the Groovy syntax as they are needed. The version used in this book is 2.0.4.

Scala

This is a fully functional language into which we will slowly transition. As with Groovy, I will explain the syntax as it is introduced. The version used in this book is 2.10.0.

Why No Java 8?

Some people might wonder why I'm not including any Java 8 right now. As of this writing, Java 7 is the currently stable and widely used version. Because I want everyone, not just early adopters, to be able to take something from this book, I thought starting from Java 7 would be most accessible.

Those using Java 8 will be able to use some of the Groovy concepts, such as higher-order functions, without actually transitioning into Groovy.

Math Notation Review

Because functional programming is so closely tied to mathematics, let's go over some basic mathematical notation.

Functions in mathematics are represented with a *name(parameters) = body* style. The example in Equation P-1 shows a very simple function. The *name* is *f*, the *parameter list* is *x*, the *body* is *x + 1*, and the *return* is the numeric result of x + 1.

Equation P-1. A simple math function

$$f(x) = x + 1$$

if statements in math are represented by the array notation. We will have a list of operations in which one will be evaluated when the corresponding if statement is true. The simple example in Equation P-2 shows a set of statements to be evaluated. The function abs(x) will return x * -1 if our x is less than 0; otherwise, it will return x.

Equation P-2. A simple math if statement

$$abs(x) = \begin{cases} x * -1 & \text{if } x < 0 \\ x & \text{else} \end{cases}$$

We also use a *summation*, the sigma operator, in our notation. The example in Equation P-3 shows a simple summation. The notation says to have a variable n starting at 0 (defined by the n=0 below the sigma) and continuing to x (as defined by the x above the sigma). Then, for each n we add it to our sum (defined by the body, n in our case, to the right of the sigma).

Equation P-3. A simple math summation

$$f(x) = \sum_{n=0}^{x} n$$

Why Functional over Imperative?

There are quite a few paradigms, each with its own pros and cons. Imperative, functional, event-driven—all of these paradigms represent another way of programming. Most people are familiar with the imperative style because it is the most common style of programming. Languages such as Java and C languages are all imperative by design. Java incorporates object-oriented programming (OOP) into its language, but it still primarily uses an imperative paradigm.

One of the most common questions I've heard during my time in software is "why should I bother learning functional programming?" Because most of my new projects have been in languages like Scala, the easiest response I can give is "that is what the project is written in." But let's take a step back and actually answer the question in depth.

I've seen quite a bit of imperative code that requires cryptographers to fully understand what it does. Generally, with the imperative style, you can write code and make it up as you go. You can write classes upon classes without fully understanding what the implementation will be. This usually results in a very large, unsustainable code base filled with an overuse of classes and spaghetti code.

Functional programming, on the other hand, forces us to better understand our implementation before and while we're coding. We can then use that to identify where abstractions should go and reduce the lines of code we have written to execute the same functionality.

Why Functional Alongside OOP?

When we think of OOP, we normally think of a paradigm that is in a class of its own. But if we look at how we write OOP, the OOP is really used for encapsulation of variables into objects. Our code is actually in the imperative style—that is, it is executed "top to bottom." As we transition to functional programming, we'll see many more instances in which we just pass function returns into other functions.

Some people see functional programming as a replacement for OOP, but in fact we'll still use OOP so that we can continue using objects that can maintain methods. These methods, hoever, will usually call static versions that allow us to have purer and more testable functions. So, we're not replacing OOP; rather, we're using object-oriented design in a functional construct.

Why Functional Programming Is Important

Concepts such as design patterns in Java are so integral to our daily programming that it's almost impossible to imagine life without them. So it is very interesting that, by contrast, the functional style has been around for many years but remains in the background as a main programming paradigm.

Why, then, is functional programming becoming so much more important today if it's been around so long? Well, think back to the dot-com era, a time when any web presence was better than none. And what about general applications? As long as the application worked, nobody cared about the language or paradigm in which it was written.

Requirements and expectations today are difficult, so being able to closely mirror mathematical functions allows engineers to design strong algorithms in advance and rely on developers to implement those algorithms within the time frame required. The closer we bind ourselves to a mathematical underpinning, the better understood our algorithms will be. Functional programming also allows us to apply mathematics on those functions. Using concepts such as derivatives, limits, and integrals on functions can be useful when we are trying to identify where functions might fail.

Large functions are not very testable and also not very readable. Often, as software developers, we find ourselves presented with large chunks of functionality thrown into one function. But, if we extract the inner workings of these large, cumbersome functions into multiple, smaller, more understandable functions, we allow for more code reuse as well as higher levels of testing.

Code reuse and higher levels of testing are two of the most important benefits of moving to a functional language. Being able to extract entire chunks of functionality from a function makes it possible for us to change the functionality later without using a copy-and-paste methodology.

Conventions Used in This Book

The following typographical conventions are used in this book:

Italic
> Indicates new terms, URLs, email addresses, filenames, and file extensions.

`Constant width`
> Used for program listings, as well as within paragraphs to refer to program elements such as variable or function names, databases, data types, environment variables, statements, and keywords.

Constant width bold

Shows commands or other text that should be typed literally by the user.

Constant width italic

Shows text that should be replaced with user-supplied values or by values determined by context.

This icon signifies a tip, suggestion, or general note.

This icon indicates a warning or caution.

Math Warning

Every now and again, I'll introduce some mathematics; I'll try to warn you beforehand. Check out the section "Math Notation Review" on page viii if you are rusty on reading mathematical notations.

Using Code Examples

Supplemental material (code examples, exercises, etc.) is available for download at *https://github.com/jbackfield/BecomingFunctional*.

This book is here to help you get your job done. In general, if example code is offered with this book, you may use it in your programs and documentation. You do not need to contact us for permission unless you're reproducing a significant portion of the code. For example, writing a program that uses several chunks of code from this book does not require permission. Selling or distributing a CD-ROM of examples from O'Reilly books does require permission. Answering a question by citing this book and quoting example code does not require permission. Incorporating a significant amount of example code from this book into your product's documentation does require permission.

We appreciate, but do not require, attribution. An attribution usually includes the title, author, publisher, and ISBN. For example: "*Becoming Functional* by Joshua Backfield (O'Reilly). Copyright 2014 Joshua Backfield, 978-1-449-36817-3."

If you feel your use of code examples falls outside fair use or the aforementioned permission, feel free to contact us at *permissions@oreilly.com*.

Safari® Books Online

 *Safari Books Online* is an on-demand digital library that delivers expert content in both book and video form from the world's leading authors in technology and business.

Technology professionals, software developers, web designers, and business and creative professionals use Safari Books Online as their primary resource for research, problem solving, learning, and certification training.

Safari Books Online offers a range of product mixes and pricing programs for organizations, government agencies, and individuals. Subscribers have access to thousands of books, training videos, and prepublication manuscripts in one fully searchable database from publishers like O'Reilly Media, Prentice Hall Professional, Addison-Wesley Professional, Microsoft Press, Sams, Que, Peachpit Press, Focal Press, Cisco Press, John Wiley & Sons, Syngress, Morgan Kaufmann, IBM Redbooks, Packt, Adobe Press, FT Press, Apress, Manning, New Riders, McGraw-Hill, Jones & Bartlett, Course Technology, and dozens more. For more information about Safari Books Online, please visit us online.

How to Contact Us

Please address comments and questions concerning this book to the publisher:

O'Reilly Media, Inc.
1005 Gravenstein Highway North
Sebastopol, CA 95472
800-998-9938 (in the United States or Canada)
707-829-0515 (international or local)
707-829-0104 (fax)

We have a web page for this book, where we list errata, examples, and any additional information. You can access this page at *http://bit.ly/becoming-functional*.

To comment or ask technical questions about this book, send email to *bookques tions@oreilly.com*.

For more information about our books, courses, conferences, and news, see our website at *http://www.oreilly.com*.

Find us on Facebook: *http://facebook.com/oreilly*

Follow us on Twitter: *http://twitter.com/oreillymedia*

Watch us on YouTube: *http://www.youtube.com/oreillymedia*

Acknowledgments

I'd like to thank my wife, Teri, and my daughter, Alyssa, for putting up with me during the writing of this book. I'd also like to thank Kevin Schmidt for introducing me to Simon St.Laurent, who made this book a reality, and my bosses, Gary Herndon and Alan Honeycutt, for allowing me to push the boundaries at work and try new things. I'd especially like to thank Meghan Blanchette, who kept moving me along and made sure that I was continuing to make progress along the way. Finally, I want to thank my parents, Sue and Fred Backfield, for believing in me and pushing me to continue learning and growing when I was a kid. If it weren't for all of you making a difference in my life, I wouldn't be here sharing my knowledge with so many other aspiring developers today.

There are lots of other people I've met along the way who have helped me become a better developer; I know I'm going to leave people out (and I'm sorry if I do), but here is a good attempt at a list: Nick Angus, Johnny Calhoun, Jason Pinkey, Ryan Karetas, Isaac Henry, Jim Williams, Mike Wisener, Yatin Kanetkar, Sean McNealy, Christopher Heath, and Dave Slusher.

CHAPTER 1

Introduction

Our first step before we get into actual examples is to look at what defines functional programming. Specifically, we will look at the components that make up functional programming and how they relate to mathematics.

 Functional programming traces its roots all the way back to LISP, although the paradigm name itself wasn't truly coined until John Backus delivered his 1977 Turing Award–winning paper "Can Programming Be Liberated From the von Neumann Style? A Functional Style and Its Algebra of Programs." In his lecture, Backus discusses multiple points about applications being built as combinations of algebraic equations.

Overview of Concepts in Functional Programming

Although there is still some disagreement about what functional programming is, there are a few features that are generally agreed to be part of it:

- First-class functions
- Pure functions
- Recursion
- Immutable variables
- Nonstrict evaluation
- Statements
- Pattern matching

First-Class Functions

First-class functions can either accept another function as an argument or return a function. Being able to create functions and return them or pass them to other functions becomes extremely useful in code reusability and code abstractions.

Pure Functions

Pure functions are functions that have no side effects. *Side effects* are actions a function may perform that are not solely contained within the function itself. When we think about side effects, we normally think about other functions, such as `println` or mutating a global variable. We can also see this when we pass in a variable and mutate it directly inside of that function.

Recursion

Recursion allows us to write smaller, more concise algorithms and to operate by looking only at the inputs to our functions. This means that our function is concerned only with the iteration it is on at the moment and whether it must continue.

Immutable Variables

Immutable variables, once set, cannot be changed. Although immutability seems very difficult to do, given the fact that the state must change within an application at some point, we'll see ways that we can accomplish it.

Nonstrict Evaluation

Nonstrict evaluations allow us to have variables that have not been computed yet. Strict evaluations—assigning a variable as soon as it is defined—are what we are used to. Nonstrict means that we can have a variable that does *not* get assigned (computed) until the first time it is referenced.

Statements

Statements are evaluable pieces of code that have a return value. Think about `if` statements that have a return value of some kind. Each line of code should be considered a statement, meaning there are very few side effects within the application itself.

Pattern Matching

Pattern matching doesn't really appear in mathematics, but assists functional programming in decreasing the need for specific variables. In code we usually encapsulate a group of variables together inside of an object. Pattern matching allows us to better type-check and extract elements from an object, making for simpler and more concise statements with less need for variable definitions.

Functional Programming and Concurrency

Concurrency enables us to do processing in parallel, and we won't cover much about it here because the topic could fill its own book. Some people believe that functional programming actually solves concurrency issues, but this is not actually the case; rather, some of the concepts of functional programming help us to create more well-defined patterns to handle concurrency.

For example, techniques such as message passing help us to create more independent threads by allowing a thread to receive messages without causing another thread to block before it is received.

In addition, features such as immutability help us to define global states and allow global state transitions as a whole rather than partial state changes or major synchronizations between threads.

Conclusion

This chapter was intended as a high-level overview of the important concepts of functional programming. At this point you're probably wondering "how can I actually get started *using* these concepts?" As we go through this book, we'll look at how to implement these features in your code.

In each chapter, I'll introduce a concept, and then we'll work to refactor and implement it in our example code for the ficticious company XXY. The examples have no "driver code." I assume that everyone reading this book can write simple Java `main()` functions to test out the code we're writing. I'm doing this for two reasons.

First, I really want you to write the code and test it out yourself; just reading the examples isn't going to help you understand the concepts or help you become a better functional programmer.

Second, I want to draw attention away from the driver code. Sometimes, when writing more extraneous code to actually call the code that we're refactoring, we either forget to refactor the driver code or tend to write too much. Would it really be useful to create a set of driver code to create 10 or 20 `Customer` objects?

Each language example is compilable and runnable. The language examples will not rely on external packages. One of the things I truly dislike about some concept books or language books is that normally the author will push you to download third-party packages. In contrast, the goal of this book is to teach you how to deal with functional concepts using the core language.

CHAPTER 2

First-Class Functions

Although most functional programming books present immutable variables first, we're going to start with first-class functions. My hope is that as you read through this chapter, you will see ways in which you could start using some of these ideas at your job tomorrow.

First-class functions are functions treated as objects themselves, meaning we can pass a function as a parameter to another function, return a function from a function, or store a function in a variable. This is one of the most useful features in functional programming, and also one of the most difficult to learn to use effectively.

Introduction to XXY

Welcome to your new company, XXY. You have been hired for your functional programming skills, which your boss would like to use in order to make the company's code more "functional." XXY currently uses Java but is interested in some newer languages such as Groovy or Scala. Although you have some ideas, you have been told that the company can't afford to just "throw away all of its current code and start over."

All right, it's time to get down to business. You have been tasked with adding a new function to return a list of enabled customers' addresses. Your boss tells you the code should be added to the *Customer.java* file, where XXY is already implementing the same type of functionality (see Example 2-1).

Example 2-1. Customer.java file contents

```java
import java.util.ArrayList;
import java.util.List;

public class Customer {

  static public ArrayList<Customer> allCustomers = new ArrayList<Customer>();
  public Integer id = 0;
```

```java
public String name = "";
public String address = "";
public String state = "";
public String primaryContact = "";
public String domain = "";
public Boolean enabled = true;

public Customer() {}

public static List<String> getEnabledCustomerNames() {
  ArrayList<String> outList = new ArrayList<String>();
    for(Customer customer : Customer.allCustomers) {
      if(customer.enabled) {
        outList.add(customer.name);
      }
    }
  return outList;
}

public static List<String> getEnabledCustomerStates() {
  ArrayList<String> outList = new ArrayList<String>();
  for(Customer customer : Customer.allCustomers) {
    if(customer.enabled) {
      outList.add(customer.state);
    }
  }
  return outList;
}

public static List<String> getEnabledCustomerPrimaryContacts() {
  ArrayList<String> outList = new ArrayList<String>();
  for(Customer customer : Customer.allCustomers) {
    if(customer.enabled) {
      outList.add(customer.primaryContact);
    }
  }
  return outList;
}

public static List<String> getEnabledCustomerDomains() {
  ArrayList<String> outList = new ArrayList<String>();
  for(Customer customer : Customer.allCustomers) {
    if(customer.enabled) {
      outList.add(customer.domain);
    }
  }
  return outList;
}

/* TODO: Add a main function */
}
```

There are four almost identical functions in the preceding example. Each function has:

- The creation of an array list
- A `for` loop
- An `if` statement
- A `return` statement

We have six lines of code duplicated per function. That's 18 lines of duplicated code: one of those functions started this, which means we have 12 lines that have been copied and pasted.

Introduction to the DRY Principle

The DRY (Don't Repeat Yourself) principle has been around for many years; the concept is that we should not be duplicating lines of code. This makes the code harder to maintain. But why is that the case?

Think about what happens if you duplicate a function multiple times. Now imagine that you just found a bug in one of those functions; you'll have to go through however many other functions to see if that same bug exists.

What would happen if you renamed `enabled`, or if you decided to deprecate the `enabled` field for something else? Now you have four functions that need to be rewritten. Could you imagine if you got a request for the alternate `getDisabled*` functions? This explodes to eight copied-and-pasted functions.

You start getting a little light-headed thinking, "What have I gotten myself into?" You take a deep breath and realize that you can do this; you're a functional programmer and eradicating copy and paste is what you do! Our first step is to begin thinking of functions as objects.

Functions as Objects

As we said before, first-class functions can be both passed and returned from another function. Let's begin by thinking about what a function is. In its most general form, a function is merely a way to encapsulate a piece of work so that we can easily reference it again—that is, nothing more than a *macro*.

What are the components of a function? Functions are made up of a *name* that is used to identify the function, a *parameter list* containing objects to operate on, a *body* where we transform the parameters, and finally a *return* to specify the result.

Let's break down the `getEnabledCustomerNames` function from the *Customer.java* file (see Example 2-2). As we can see, the function name is `getEnabledCustomerNames`, the parameter list is `empty`, and the body contains code that iterates over the `Customer.all Customers` list, adding the `customer.name` field to an output list only if the customer is enabled. Finally, our return is our output list, `outList`.

Example 2-2. Customer.getEnabledCustomerNames

```
public static List<String> getEnabledCustomerNames() {
  ArrayList<String> outList = new ArrayList<String>();
  for(Customer customer : Customer.allCustomers) {
    if(customer.enabled) {
      outList.add(customer.name);
    }
  }
  return outList;
}
```

Refactoring Using If-Else Structures

Let's write a new function that performs the same functionality from Example 2-2 (excluding the addition of the field to the `outList`) and call it `getEnabledCustomer Field`. For the moment, we'll just add a comment `//Placeholder` where we were grabbing the `customer.name` field and appending it to `outList`.

The first thing to do is to create a new `ArrayList` at the top of our function:

```
public static List<String> getEnabledCustomerField() {
  ArrayList<String> outList = new ArrayList<String>();
```

We then create the `for` loop and the `if` statement, which checks for the customer being enabled:

```
for(Cutomer customer : Customer.allCustomers) {
  if(customer.enabled) {
```

As I mentioned, we're going to put in a placeholder where we were originally appending the field value to our list. We then close out the `if` structure and `for` loop, returning the new `outList`:

```
    //Placeholder
    }
  }
  return outList;
}
```

Let's put all of this together to create our new `getEnabledCustomerField` method, as shown in Example 2-3.

Example 2-3. getEnabledCustomerField with placeholder

```
public static List<String> getEnabledCustomerField() {
  ArrayList<String> outList = new ArrayList<String>();
  for(Customer customer : Customer.allCustomers) {
    if(customer.enabled) {
      //Placeholder
    }
  }
  return outList;
}
```

Because we know all the possible fields that we're looking for, let's take a new parameter, the field name we're looking for. We'll then add an `if` structure to append our list with the value of the field we are looking for, as shown in Example 2-4.

Example 2-4. getEnabledCustomerField with if structure

```
public static List<String> getEnabledCustomerField(String field) {
  ArrayList<String> outList = new ArrayList<String>();
  for(Customer customer : Customer.allCustomers) {
    if(customer.enabled) {
      if(field == "name") {
        outList.add(customer.name);
      } else if(field == "state") {
        outList.add(customer.state);
      } else if(field == "primaryContact") {
        outList.add(customer.primaryContact);
      } else if(field == "domain") {
        outList.add(customer.domain);
      } else if(field == "address") {
        outList.add(customer.address);
      } else {
        throw new IllegalArgumentException("Unknown field");
      }
    }
  }
  return outList;
}
```

Type Safety by Exception

In Example 2-4, we're throwing an `IllegalArgumentException` to ensure type safety. This means that we are throwing an exception if the field is not one of our predefined fields.

Why is this such a bad idea? You are avoiding type safety since you are relying on string comparisons for field accessors. You are also now relying on someone spelling it correctly *both* in the `if` structure as well as when he calls the method itself.

There are other ways to ensure type safety, such as using enumerations containing a list of valid values and matching the corresponding enumeration in our `if/else` structure.

OK, we've just consolidated the *looping* functionality to exist in only one function. So what happens if we keep adding fields to extract? We'll keep adding field checks to the `if/else` structure, which means we'll eventually end up with an unmanageable `if` structure. What if we could provide a simple function to extract the field we want from the object itself?

Refactoring Using Function Objects to Extract Fields

We're going to be using Java interfaces to create an abstraction of a function that we could pass to another function. Many other languages, including the proposals in Java 8, offer functions as objects; as of this writing, however, Java 7 is the currently released and stable version. Thus, we are going to use interfaces to create functionality that we can pass to other functions.

You might be familiar with the `Runnable` interface, with which you encapsulate some function that you want to execute on a thread. We have similar functionality here, except we need a function that can take an object (the object from which we want to extract a field) and return an object (the value of the field).

Math Warning

Let's assume that we have a function, f, that does some computation referencing the function a and returns the value:

$$f(x) = x^2 / a(x)$$

Now, let's assume that we want to rewrite f so that instead of calling a we call b. Well, to continue rewriting these functions as f and f' (and so on) would be duplication. Lambda calculus introduced the concept of *passing* a function to a function. So, instead of calling the function a, what if we could pass it in? Let's redefine f:

$$f(x, c) = x^2 / c(x)$$

Now, we can make a call into our function using either a or b fairly easily. Let's see the call and substitute our values:

$$f(20, a) = 20^2 / a(20)$$

What should our function take as an argument? Let's look where it will be called. It will be replacing the giant `if` structure. The purpose of our function is to *convert* a Customer record into a String, which means our new function will *take* a Customer object and *return* a String. Let's build our interface definition.

The first thing that we do is give our interface a name:

```
private interface ConversionFunction {
```

Next we'll define our method, which is the entry point into our *function*. As I said before, it will take a Customer and return a String:

```
  public String call(Customer customer);
}
```

Example 2-5 shows the entirety of the ConversionFunction definition.

Example 2-5. ConversionFunction definition

```
private interface ConversionFunction {
  public String call(Customer customer);
}
```

We'll want to make this interface public later, moving it into its own file and making it a little more generic. But for now, let's focus on using this new ConversionFunction interface by replacing our giant `if` structure.

First, we replace the field parameter with a `ConversionFunction` object. We can then replace the giant `if`/`else` structure with a call to `func.call(customer)`. Remember, the `call` method inside the `ConversionFunction` interface will be performing the conversion for us. All we need to do is execute `call` and add the result. Check out the code in Example 2-6.

Example 2-6. getEnabledCustomerField definition with ConversionFunction

```
public static List<String> getEnabledCustomerField(ConversionFunction func) {
  ArrayList<String> outList = new ArrayList<String>();
  for(Customer customer : Customer.allCustomers) {
    if(customer.enabled) {
      outList.add(func.call(customer));
    }
  }
  return outList;
}
```

Now that we're starting to think more functionally, let's see what one of those `ConversionFunctions` would look like. Just return the field that you want to extract. In the following example, the `CustomerAddress` class allows us to take a `Customer` and return the `address` field:

```
static private class CustomerAddress implements ConversionFunction {
  public String call(Customer customer) { return customer.address; }
}
```

Let's go ahead and make your boss happy now by implementing the `getEnabledCustomerAddresses` function he wanted. We can create our `getEnabledCustomerAddresses` function, which will call our new `getEnabledCustomerField` method and pass it a conversion function. Now if the definition of `enabled` ever changes, we only have to fix it in one place:

```
public static List<String> getEnabledCustomerAddresses() {
  return Customer.getEnabledCustomerField(new CustomerAddress());
}
```

Although we don't need to do it yet, what would happen if we needed to get a list of all enabled customers? Well, our current interface really doesn't help there, because our interface is strictly defined to take a `Customer` object and return a `String`. We should modify our interface to be more abstract by using generic typing. Let's start by renaming our `ConversionFunction` to `Function1`, taking two type parameters (`A1` and `B`, which are the type of the parameter and the return, respectively). Our new function is shown in Example 2-7.

Example 2-7. Interface for encapsulating a function taking one argument

```
public interface Function1<A1,B> {
  public B call(A1 in1);
}
```

Type Parameter Naming Convention

Why are we naming this interface `Function1`? Well, we're naming it `Function` because it is going to be wrapping a function. The number 1 comes from the number of parameters that the function itself will take. Our generic typing seems a little odd because we have two parameters, but remember that the final parameter is the *return* type.

So, what if we needed a function that takes two arguments (shown in Example 2-8) or four arguments (shown in Example 2-9)?

Example 2-8. Interface for encapsulating a function taking two arguments

```
public interface Function2<A1,A2,B> {
  public B call(A1, in1,A2 in2);
}
```

Example 2-9. Interface for encapsulating a function taking four arguments

```
public interface Function4<A1,A2,A3,A4,B> {
  public B call(A1 in1,A2 in2,A3 in3,A4 in4);
}
```

Next, we'll update the `CustomerAddress` inheritance to be `Function1<Custom er,String>`.

```
  static private class CustomerAddress implements Function1<Customer, String> {
    public String call(Customer customer) { return customer.address; }
  }
```

We then update `getEnabledCustomerField` to take a `Function1`. Our first parameter will always be a `Customer`, but our second parameter will change, so we'll leave that as B. We then parameterize the `getEnabledCustomerField` method to take a parameter B and finally update our return type for `getEnabledCustomerField` to return a `List` of type B (see Example 2-10).

Example 2-10. getEnabledCustomerField with generic typed Function1

```
public static <B> List<B> getEnabledCustomerField(Function1<Customer,B> func) {
  ArrayList<B> outList = new ArrayList<B>();
  for(Customer customer : Customer.allCustomers) {
    if(customer.enabled) {
      outList.add(func.call(customer));
    }
  }
}
```

```
        return outList;
}
```

Now that you've done what your boss asked, it's time to convert all the other getEna
bledCustomer* functions. We'll just create a new class that implements our Func
tion1 interface and then update the getEnabledCustomer* method to call the Custom
er.getEnabledCustomerField() method with a new instance of the appropriate class.
Go ahead and refactor the rest of the file and then check out the code in Example 2-11
to see how it looks.

Example 2-11. Customer.java file after initial refactoring

```java
import java.util.ArrayList;
import java.util.List;

public class Customer {

    static public ArrayList<Customer> allCustomers = new ArrayList<Customer>();
    public Integer id = 0;
    public String name = "";
    public String address = "";
    public String state = "";
    public String primaryContact = "";
    public String domain = "";
    public Boolean enabled = true;

    public Customer() {}

    private interface Function1<A1,B> {
      public B call(A1 in1);
    }

    static private class CustomerAddress implements Function1<Customer, String> {
      public String call(Customer customer) { return customer.address; }
    }

    static private class CustomerName implements Function1<Customer, String> {
      public String call(Customer customer) { return customer.name; }
    }

    static private class CustomerState implements Function1<Customer, String> {
      public String call(Customer customer) { return customer.state; }
    }

    static private class CustomerPrimaryContact implements Function1<Customer, String>
    {
      public String call(Customer customer) { return customer.primaryContact; }
    }

    static private class CustomerDomain implements Function1<Customer, String> {
      public String call(Customer customer) { return customer.domain; }
```

```
    }

    static private class CustomerAsCustomer implements Function1<Customer, Customer> {
      public String call(Customer customer) { return customer; }
    }

    public static List<String> getEnabledCustomerAddresses() {
      return Customer.getEnabledCustomerField(new CustomerAddress());
    }

    public static List<String> getEnabledCustomerNames() {
      return Customer.getEnabledCustomerField(new CustomerName());
    }

    public static List<String> getEnabledCustomerStates() {
      return Customer.getEnabledCustomerField(new CustomerState());
    }

    public static List<String> getEnabledCustomerPrimaryContacts() {
      return Customer.getEnabledCustomerField(new CustomerPrimaryContact());
    }

    public static List<String> getEnabledCustomerDomains() {
      return Customer.getEnabledCustomerField(new CustomerDomain());
    }

    public static <B> List<B> getEnabledCustomerField(Function1<Customer,B> func) {
      ArrayList<B> outList = new ArrayList<B>();
      for(Customer customer : Customer.allCustomers) {
        if(customer.enabled) {
          outList.add(func.call(customer));
        }
      }
      return outList;
    }
}
```

Let's answer our original question of "what would happen if we needed to get a list of all enabled customers?" We can create a new class that takes a customer and returns a customer, as shown in Example 2-12.

Example 2-12. A Customer as Customer class

```
static private class CustomerAsCustomer implements Function1<Customer, Customer> {
  public String call(Customer customer) { return customer; }
}
```

Now, we can call Customer.getEnabledCustomerField(new CustomerAsCusto
mer()), which gives us a list of all our enabled cutomers. But what if we didn't want to
have to create all of these *named* classes? What if we didn't actually need to define full
classes? Well, that leads right into the next section on anonymous functions.

Anonymous Functions

Anonymous functions are split into two types: lambda functions and closures. Closures are quite similar to lambdas with a very subtle difference, which we'll discuss later. As you learned in the previous section, functions are made up of four parts: name, parameter list, body, and return. But what if we didn't need the name of the function? This is the idea behind anonymous functions: being able to create functions that have a limited scope and need to exist only for a short time.

Math Warning

Let's bring back our function from the beginning of this chapter:

$$f(x, c) = x^2 / c(x)$$

Lambda calculus enables us to create a function without defining it formally. Our function f is a formal definition, but what if we want to pass in a function as the parameter c for something really simple, such as a square of the input? Let's see that and substitute our variables:

$$f(10, y \rightarrow y^2) = 10^2 / (y \rightarrow y^2)(10)$$

The lambda expression is a function that takes an x parameter and performs the x^2 operation. So when we substitute, we can actually replace the entire c(x) definition with the lambda function itself. Let's simplify the function call a little bit, since we can now evaluate our lambda function:

$$f(10, y \rightarrow y^2) = 10^2 / 10^2$$

Back at XXY, your boss is excited to see the company's code becoming "functional." However, he's concerned with the number of extra classes being created and feels they are unnecessary. He's asked you to clean up the code by reducing the number of inner classes. Luckily, we can do this by using lambda functions.

Lambda Functions

Lambda functions are *unnamed* functions that contain a parameter list, a body, and a return. In the following `getEnabledCustomerAddresses` example, let's try to use an anonymous function (in this case, an anonymous instance of `Function1`) to get rid of the superfluous `CustomerAddress` class:

```
new Function1<Customer, String>() {
  public String call(Customer customer) { return customer.address; }
}
```

Let's use this anonymous class by sending it to our getEnabledCustomerField function (see Example 2-13). We can now remove the CustomerAddress conversion class.

Example 2-13. getEnabledCustomerAddresses using anonymous Function1

```
public static List<String> getEnabledCustomerAddresses() {
  return Customer.getEnabledCustomerField(new Function1<Customer,String>() {
    public String call(Customer customer) { return customer.address; }
  });
}
```

Go ahead and see if you can refactor the rest of the functions; when you're done, check out Example 2-14 and see how they compare.

Example 2-14. Customer.java file with anonymous classes

```
import java.util.ArrayList;
import java.util.List;

public class Customer {

  static public ArrayList<Customer> allCustomers = new ArrayList<Customer>();
  public Integer id = 0;
  public String name = "";
  public String address = "";
  public String state = "";
  public String primaryContact = "";
  public String domain = "";
  public Boolean enabled = true;

  public Customer() {}

  private interface Function1<A1,B> {
    public B call(A1 in1);
  }

  public static List<String> getEnabledCustomerAddresses() {
    return Customer.getEnabledCustomerField(new Function1<Customer,String>() {
      public String call(Customer customer) { return customer.addresses; }
    });
  }

  public static List<String> getEnabledCustomerNames() {
    return Customer.getEnabledCustomerField(new Function1<Customer, String>() {
      public String call(Customer customer) { return customer.name; }
    });
  }

  public static List<String> getEnabledCustomerStates() {
```

```
    return Customer.getEnabledCustomerField(new Function1<Customer, String>() {
      public String call(Customer customer) { return customer.state; }
    });
  }

  public static List<String> getEnabledCustomerPrimaryContacts() {
    return Customer.getEnabledCustomerField(new Function1<Customer, String>() {
      public String call(Customer customer) { return customer.primaryContact; }
    });
  }

  public static List<String> getEnabledCustomerDomains() {
    return Customer.getEnabledCustomerField(new Function1<Customer, String>() {
      public String call(Customer customer) { return customer.domain; }
    });
  }

  public static <B> List<B> getEnabledCustomerField(Function1<Customer,B> func) {
    ArrayList<B> outList = new ArrayList<B>();
    for(Customer customer : Customer.allCustomers) {
      if(customer.enabled) {
        outList.add(func.call(customer));
      }
    }
    return outList;
  }
}
```

Your boss is excited by how great a job you're doing, but he now needs a new piece of functionality. He needs to have his email prepended to the domain of each Customer. As with most strange requests, you just kind of stare blankly at him for a moment and then agree to carry it out.

Your boss then shows you an example of a Customer with the domain *xxy.com*, which is already defined in the Customer object. "You should be able to just concatenate my email with the domain of each Customer object and be done," he says. "Something like *boss@xxy.com*." You think for a few minutes and realize that it is a perfect time to use closures!

Closures

Closures are much like lambdas, except they reference variables outside the scope of the function. In the simplest explanation, the body references a variable that doesn't exist in either the body or the parameter list.

Your boss's request to prepend his email onto customer domains seems like a really simple function to write. We're going to use our getEnabledCustomerField, and in our anonymous function we'll prepend "boss@" to the customer domains:

```
public static List<String> getEnabledCustomerBossesEmail() {
    return Customer.getEnabledCustomerField(new Function1<Customer, String>() {
        public String call(Customer customer) {
            return "boss@" + customer.domain;
        }
    });
}
```

But wait—what happens if the president of XXY comes to you and says, "I want my email prepended to the customer domains"? The first idea that comes to you is to copy and paste the function and update it with "president@". This violates the DRY principle, however, so you should reconsider this approach. What if we were able to bring in a variable that was outside of our class definition? Well, this is a perfect use of a closure.

We know that we're going to have a name of someone passed into our function getEna bledCustomerSomeoneEmail. This function should have a variable, someone, passed to it. At this point, we can reference the someone variable from inside our anonymous function and create the email address (see Example 2-15).

Example 2-15. getEnabledCustomerSomeoneEmail with final field

```
public static List<String> getEnabledCustomerSomeoneEmail(final String someone) {
    return Customer.getEnabledCustomerField(new Function1<Customer, String>() {
        public String call(Customer customer) {
            return someone + "@" + customer.domain;
        }
    });
}
```

 Remember to Mark Closed-Over Variables as final
Always remember to mark closed-over variables as final. The Java compiler requires this; otherwise, it will throw a compile-time error of local variable someone is accessed from within inner class: needs to be declared final.

This is still a real closure, which we can tell from Example 2-16. Notice that we have our original Closure variable coming in; we can see the variable printed out (providing us a variable reference) and the contents (which should be a blank string). Next, we set the internal string variable to bar and then create/run our closure (it is a closure because the scope of the t variable is "closed over" and brought into the scope of our runnable).

Upon execution, we print out "bar" as is expected, but notice that the reference is the same! We then set the internal string to baz and exit our closure. The next line in our function is to print out the internal string, which is now "baz" and still has the same reference. Although a very simple example, this is a perfect illustration of how a closure truly works; we have an internal function that closes over a variable outside of its normal scope.

Example 2-16. A closure in Java showing that the variable is actually closed over

```java
public class Closure {

  public String foo = "";

  public static Closure process(final Closure t) {
    System.out.println(t.toString() + " = " + t.foo);
    t.foo = "bar";
    new Runnable() {
      public void run() {
        System.out.println(t.toString() + " = " + t.foo);
        t.foo = "baz";
      }
    }.run();
    System.out.println(t.toString() + " = " + t.foo);
    return t;
  }

  public static void main(String[] args) {
    process(new Closure());
  }

}
```

Using closures, you can build functions and pass them to other functions while referencing local variables. Think about our example of specifying any name to prepend to customer domains. If we were unable to close over the local variable of someone, we would be forced to create new functions for every name we wanted to prepend. This means we would have quite a bit more code duplication.

Higher-Order Functions

The day you have been dreading has come: your boss has asked you to re-create the functions getEnabledCustomerAddresses, getEnabledCustomerNames, getEnabled CustomerStates, getEnabledCustomerPrimaryContacts, and getEnabledCustomer Domains as getDisabled style functions. The first way of doing this is to copy and paste the .getEnabledCustomerField method and create a .getDisabledField changing if (customer.enabled) to if (!customer.enabled), as shown in Example 2-17.

Example 2-17. getDisabledField

```java
public static <B> List<B> getDisabledField(Function1<Customer,B> func) {
  ArrayList<B> outList = new ArrayList<B>();
  for(Customer customer : Customer.allCustomers) {
    if (!customer.enabled) {
      outList.add(func.call(customer));
    }
  }
```

```
  return outList;
}
```

It should be obvious that, again, we are violating the DRY principle. Let's extract the test functionality in the if statement so that we can pass it into the function. We will accept a function taking a Customer and returning a Boolean that will tell us whether it should be included. We then replace our if with the evaluation of the test function call (see Example 2-18).

Example 2-18. getField with test function

```
public static <B> List<B> getField(Function1<Customer,Boolean> test,
                                    Function1<Customer,B> func) {
  ArrayList<B> outList = new ArrayList<B>();
  for (Customer customer : Customer.allCustomers) {
    if (test.call(customer)) {
      outList.add(func.call(customer));
    }
  }
  return outList;
}
```

Now, at first glance, we see that with this approach we're going to be copying and pasting a ton of anonymous functions for each function. Instead, we'll create two variables in which we will store the Enabled and Disabled Function1 implementations.

Inside of our Customer class, we'll create two function variables, EnabledCustomer and DisabledCustomer. This allows us to apply the DRY principle by not rewriting our Enabled and Disabled function implementations:

```
static final public Function1<Customer,Boolean> EnabledCustomer =
                                      new Function1<Customer,Boolean>()
{
  public Boolean call(Customer customer) {
    return customer.enabled == true;
  }
};

static final public Function1<Customer,Boolean> DisabledCustomer =
                                      new Function1<Customer,Boolean>()
{
  public Boolean call(Customer customer) {
    return customer.enabled == false;
  }
};
```

What does a call to this look like? Let's look at the following getDisabledCustomer Names function to see that we just pass the DisabledCustomers object as the first parameter:

```
public static List<String> getDisabledCustomerNames() {
  return Customer.getField(
    Customer.DisabledCustomers,
    new Function1<Customer, String>() {
      public String call(Customer customer) {
      return customer.name;
      }
    }
  );
}
```

As you can see, each of our `getCustomer*` methods looks a little nasty. Normally in functional programming, we wouldn't have all of these `getCustomer*` methods; instead, we would call the `Customer.getField` method where we needed the call. In the instance where we are making multiple calls over the code base—for example, if we called `get DisabledCustomerNames` in a few different places—we would then create a method encapsulating that call (think DRY).

Refactoring get Functions by Using Groovy

Let's look at an example in Groovy to see how we could implement `getDisabledCusto merNames` and `getEnabledCustomerNames` in a more functional language. Example 2-19 shows these two pieces of functionality.

Notice that we are able to use the `findAll` function, which allows you to filter a list based on another function, as we did with our `for` with the inner `if` structure inside `get Field`. We then use the `collect` method to convert one object into another, as we did with our `Function1` passed into the `getField`.

Example 2-19. getEnabledCustomerNames and getDisabledCustomerNames functions in Groovy

```
// Get all enabled customer names
allCustomers.findAll(
  { customer -> customer.enabled == true }
).collect(
  { customer -> customer.name }
)

// Get all disabled customer names
allCustomers.findAll(
  { customer -> customer.enabled == false }
).collect(
  { customer -> customer.name }
)
```

Groovy Syntax

There are a couple of things to note about our code in Example 2-19.

- There is no need for the keyword `return`. Groovy uses the last statement in a function as the return of that function.
- An anonymous function is composed of curly braces, {}, with an arrow, ->. To the left of the arrow is the parameter list, and to the right is the body of the function.
- No semicolons are necessary when you are writing in Groovy.

The big thing you'll notice is that we've reiterated ourselves with the `allCusto mers.findAll(...).collect(...)` call; and while we might say that this is duplicated code, it is a very minimal duplication in which we are actually being more expressive. If you remember back in `getDisabledCustomerNames`, the amount of code required to get the names was much higher than in our Groovy code, and not as readable.

A function becomes "higher order" if it accepts or returns a function. Because functions are not objects in Java, it does not have the concept of a higher-order function. But, in our interface equivalency, we can see that the higher-order function is actually `get Field` from Example 2-18 because it accepts a "function." In Example 2-19, we can see that the functions `findAll` and `collect` are both higher order because they themselves accept functions.

Why are higher-order functions so important? Think about the functions as objects: if we are able to pass functions as objects (without wrapping them in objects), we must have higher-order functions. Otherwise, what would utilize those functions as objects?

Conclusion

At this point, you should have an idea of how use first-class functions. In our examples, we made our new code functional and then went back and migrated our pre-existing code to the functional style. You should always remember that *any time is a good time to make code more functional.*

We took a little extra time to refactor our copy-and-paste code into a higher-order function that iterated over our list of customers. After that, we refactored the inner workings of our copy-and-paste code into simple, anonymous functions and even used a closure in case our boss ever wants to extend the functionality of the prepending email addresses.

The more we converted our copy-and-paste code using these functional concepts, the simpler our code became. It also became much easier for us to add new functionality because we no longer had to copy and paste things like our `for` loops or other pieces that we extracted into our higher-order function `getField`.

You don't always need 10 functions to cover every possible use case in the future. Of course, if `getEnabledCustomerNames` were to happen 5 or 10 times, it might make sense to create the function itself and make it a call to be done such that people aren't duplicating that code.

Many of these abstractions, such as our `Function1`, are already defined in libraries like Guava. For those of you who can't switch to a language like Groovy, I would suggest looking into these types of libraries, which already have these abstractions available.

Further Reading

The next time you are reading a programming language book, be on the lookout for how you might be able to implement higher-order functions in that language. All languages can do some form of function passing, even C (using function pointers).

CHAPTER 3

Pure Functions

We use functions to perform specific tasks and then combine them to build our applications. Each function is designed to do some work, given a set of inputs. When we don't return the result of our execution but rather mutate another external (i.e., not contained within the function scope) object, we call this a *side effect*. *Pure functions*, on the other hand, are functions that have no side effects and always perform the same computation, resulting in the same output, given a set of inputs. Although most of this seems straightforward, the implementation is quite another story.

Functions performing large amounts of work are difficult to test. Generally, to allow for your code to grow over time, you need to be able to change functionality. This means the larger your function becomes, the more parameters you need in order to modify the functionality. You should break up the function into smaller functions. These smaller functions can then be pure, allowing for a better understanding of the code's overall functionality. When a function is pure, we say that "output depends on input."

Output Depends on Input

If we pass a set of parameters into a pure function, we will *always* get the same result. The return is solely dependent on the parameter list.

Don't Closures Break Function Purity?

If we pass a closure, aren't we then dependent on the external (closed-over) variable? This is an interesting point, so let's think about closures and how they work. Closures work by bringing the closed-over variable into the scope of the function. Because the variable becomes part of the function as we pass it to another function, everything the receiving function needs to operate has been passed to the function locally.

Math Warning

Let's think about the following example:

$$f(x) = \sum_{n=0}^{100} n + x$$

Here is the key: it does not matter *what* we pass in; we can always predict the output.

Back at XXY, your boss has asked you to add a function that can update a `Contract` record and set it to `enabled`. He said there was already a function that could update a `Contract` by setting it to `disabled` by a customer. Right now, `Customers` have only one `Contract`, so that makes things a little simpler for us. Let's look at Example 3-1.

Example 3-1. Current Contract.java code

```java
import java.util.Calendar;

public class Contract {

  public Calendar begin_date;
  public Calendar end_date;
  public Boolean enabled = true;

  public Contract(Calendar begin_date) {
    this.begin_date = begin_date;
    this.end_date = this.begin_date.getInstance();
    this.end_date.setTimeInMillis(this.begin_date.getTimeInMillis());
    this.end_date.add(Calendar.YEAR, 2);
  }

  public static void setContractDisabledForCustomer(Integer customer_id) {
    for(Customer customer : Customer.allCustomers) {
      if(customer.id == customer_id) {
        customer.contract.enabled = false;
      }
    }
  }

}
```

But wait—we're using another for loop. You should remember from the previous chapter that we need to extract some of this functionality. It is likely we'll have other times when we need to get a customer by `id`.

Let's start by creating the `getCustomerById` method in the `Customer` class. We just need some basic functionality that can return the customer if it exists and return `null` if it doesn't. For now, let's check the code in Example 3-2. Inside our function is a `for` loop that iterates over the customer list; we don't want this because we have already written a loop over the `allCustomer` list. Don't worry: for many people this is how you would generally write it.

Example 3-2. getCustomerById method

```java
public static Customer getCustomerById(Integer customer_id) {
  for(Customer customer : Customer.allCustomers) {
    if(customer.id == customer_id) {
      return customer;
    }
  }
  return null;
}
```

Nullity allows us to represent the absence of a value, but using it can cause many different issues. Why is nullity considered bad? Well, if we call into `getCustomerById` and get back a `null`, what does that mean to the caller? Does that mean that we errored out? Does it mean that we were unable to find it? Think about how many places you now have to check for a `null` return value, and consider the amount of code necessary to make sure that the application does not crash with a `NullPointerException`. What other options do we have to handle our cases?

We could throw an exception if we were unable to find the `Customer` object. The problem with that is that we are telling the caller that we will throw an exception if there is no user, even though it's not actually an error.

We could also return a list *containing* the customer, or an empty list if it doesn't exist. This means that no matter what happens, we have a valid object that can be operated on at all times. Now, our caller can decide how she wants to handle the case in which the customer doesn't exist. Let's look at the code in Example 3-3.

Example 3-3. getCustomerById returning a list

```java
public static ArrayList<Customer> getCustomerById(Integer customer_id) {
  ArrayList<Customer> outList = new ArrayList<Customer>();
  for(Customer customer : Customer.allCustomers) {
    if(customer.id == customer_id) {
      outList.add(customer);
    }
  }
  return outList;
}
```

But wait a second, that `for` loop looks quite familiar. Our function *filters* or *finds all* of the customers given a `customer_id`. Remember in the preceding chapter how our method `getField` had a similar `for` loop?

Let's not repeat ourselves; instead, let's abstract that for loop into its own function, which we'll call filter. It will take a function that takes a Customer and returns a Boolean. The Boolean will indicate to us whether to keep the record. Our new function is listed in Example 3-4.

Example 3-4. filter function

```
public static ArrayList<Customer> filter(Function1<Customer, Boolean> test) {
  ArrayList<Customer> outList = new ArrayList<Customer>();
  for(Customer customer : Customer.allCustomers) {
    if(test.call(customer)) {
      outList.add(customer);
    }
  }
  return outList;
}
```

Now that we've created this function, let's think back to the getField function in our Customer object. We can actually extract the filtering functionality and use our new filter function. So, let's refactor this function—we're not going to rename it, because it's the same functionality; instead, we're extracting the filtering logic out, as shown in Example 3-5. Now we call into Customer.filter(test) and then iterate over the return of that result.

Example 3-5. getField function using a filter function

```
public static <B> List<B> getField(Function1<Customer,Boolean> test,
                                   Function1<Customer,B> func) {
  ArrayList<B> outList = new ArrayList<B>();
    for(Customer customer : Customer.filter(test)) {
      outList.add(func.call(customer));
    }
  return outList;
}
```

We also modify our getCustomerById function to use the new filter method by passing a new test function, which takes a Customer and returns a Boolean to filter by the requested customer_id, as shown in Example 3-6.

Example 3-6. getCustomerById method using filter

```
public static ArrayList<Customer> getCustomerById(final Integer customer_id) {
  return Customer.filter(new Function1<Customer, Boolean>() {
    public Boolean call(Customer customer) {
      return customer.id == customer_id;
    }
  });
}
```

Now let's return to the `Contract` class and use our `getCustomerById` function. We'll go ahead and grab our list of customers and iterate over it, setting the contract to en abled. There's no need to check that we didn't return `null`; the fact that the list will be populated with something implicitly handles the "if there are no records" issue (see Example 3-7).

Example 3-7. setContractEnabledForCustomer

```
public static void setContractEnabledForCustomer(Integer customer_id) {
  for(Customer customer : Customer.getCustomerById(customer_id)) {
    customer.contract.enabled = true;
  }
}
```

Purifying Our Functions

The first function we'll make pure is our `filter` function. We purify a function by making sure that it isn't referencing anything outside of its function arguments. This means that our reference to `Customer.allCustomers` needs to go away, and instead we should pass it in as an argument.

As our functions become more pure, it becomes easier to troubleshoot them because all of our inputs are known. In turn, because all of our inputs are known, all possible outcomes should be derivable. If they are all derivable, we should be able to determine what caused failures in logic. Obviously, our calls to the `filter` function will receive `Customer.allCustomers`, which is listed directly below the `filter` function in Example 3-8.

Example 3-8. filter function and its callers

```
public static ArrayList<Customer> filter(ArrayList<Customer> inList,
                                         Function1<Customer, Boolean> test) {
  ArrayList<Customer> outList = new ArrayList<Customer>();
  for(Customer customer : inList) {
    if(test.call(customer)) {
      outList.add(customer);
    }
  }
  return outList;
}

public static <B> List<B> getField(Function1<Customer,Boolean> test,
                                    Function1<Customer,B> func) {
  ArrayList<B> outList = new ArrayList<B>();
  for(Customer customer : Customer.filter(Customer.allCustomers, test)) {
    outList.add(func.call(customer));
  }
  return outList;
}
```

```
public static ArrayList<Customer> getCustomerById(final Integer customer_id) {
  return Customer.filter(Customer.allCustomers, new Function1<Customer, Boolean>() {
    public Boolean call(Customer customer) {
      return customer.id == customer_id;
    }
  });
}
```

Let's continue by making getCustomerById pure (see Example 3-9). This means that the method getCustomerById inside *Customer.java* must be updated to accept our customer list. This way, we no longer reference the Customer.allCustomers object directly.

Example 3-9. getCustomerById

```
public static ArrayList<Customer> getCustomerById(ArrayList<Customer> inList,
                                                  final Integer customer_id) {
  return Customer.filter(inList, new Function1<Customer, Boolean>() {
    public Boolean call(Customer customer) {
      return customer.id == customer_id;
    }
  });
}
```

We should also update setContractEnabledForCustomer to pass in Customer.allCustomers (see Example 3-10). At this point, we no longer need to have allCustomers passed in because this method only ever operates on the Customer.allCustomers object.

Example 3-10. setContractEnabledForCustomer

```
public static void setContractEnabledForCustomer(Integer customer_id) {
  for(Customer customer : Customer.getCustomerById(Customer.allCustomers,
                                                   customer_id)) {
    customer.contract.enabled = true;
  }
}
```

We need to have a method so that we can execute the customer.contract.enabled = true code *for each* object without needing to duplicate these loops. The first thing that we need to do is create a new interface, which we'll call Foreach1.

Foreach1 will be an abstraction for a higher-order function which takes an A1 and has a void return type, because we really don't care what type is being returned. In our instance, we're not returning anything because we're just setting contract.enabled = true. Check out the code for our Foreach1 interface in Example 3-11 and the Function1 interface in Example 3-12.

Refactoring Time

We should move the `Foreach1` and `Function1` interface definitions into their own *Foreach1.java* and *Function1.java* files, respectively.

Example 3-11. Foreach1.java interface definition

```
public interface Foreach1<A1> {
  public void call(A1 in1);
}
```

Example 3-12. Function1.java interface definition

```
public interface Function1<A1,B> {
  public B call(A1 in1);
}
```

We can then update the `Customer` class to have its own `foreach` function that will execute `func` for each record in the `inList`, as shown in Example 3-13.

Example 3-13. foreach function defined in the Customer class

```
public static void foreach(ArrayList<Customer> inList, Foreach1<Customer> func) {
  for(Customer customer : inList) {
    func.call(customer);
  }
}
```

We can now use our `foreach` function. For the `inList`, we're going to use a `getCusto merById`, which will return a list containing our `Customer` if it exists. For the `func`, we're going to create a new `Function1` that sets the `Contract` to enabled. You can see the code in Example 3-14.

Example 3-14. setContractEnabledForCustomer method

```
public static void setContractEnabledForCustomer(Integer customer_id) {
  Customer.foreach(
    Customer.getCustomerById(Customer.allCustomers, customer_id),
    new Foreach1<Customer>() {
      public void call(Customer customer) {
        customer.contract.enabled = true;
      }
    }
  );
}
```

Unfortunately, this code modifies the `customer` argument and sets the `customer.con tract.enabled` field. We'll address how we might fix this when we start looking at immutable variables.

Returning an Empty List Rather Than Null

In Example 3-14, notice that we're able to pass the list that was returned by `getCustomerById` directly to `foreach`. This has the nice side effect that we don't need to do null checking. The `foreach` takes care of "what happens if it doesn't exist?"

Groovy Version of setContractEnabledForCustomer

The following code shows a simple way to accomplish the same functionality we've just implemented, but in Groovy. Notice that we use `findAll`, which returns a list, and we call `each` to set `contract.enabled = true`.

```
def setContractEnabledForCustomer(Integer customer_id) {
  list.findAll(
    { customer -> customer.id == customer_id }
  ).each(
    { customer -> customer.contract.enabled = true }
  )
}
```

Now, we can easily create a `setContractDisabledForCustomer` method, as shown in Example 3-15. It's the same as Example 3-14, except for the value we're setting on `enabled` (`true` versus `false`, respectively).

Example 3-15. setContractDisabledForCustomer

```
public static void setContractDisabledForCustomer(Integer customer_id) {
  Customer.foreach(
    Customer.getCustomerById(Customer.allCustomers, customer_id),
    new Foreach1<Customer>() {
      public void call(Customer customer) {
        customer.contract.enabled = false;
      }
    }
  );
}
```

Can you think of how we can refactor both of the `setContract*ForCustomer` methods into a single function? Check out the code in Example 3-16 after you've tried it yourself.

Example 3-16. setContractForCustomer with status passed in

```
public static void setContractForCustomer(Integer customer_id, final Boolean status)
{
  Customer.foreach(
    Customer.getCustomerById(Customer.allCustomers, customer_id),
                    new Foreach1<Customer>() {
```

```
      public void call(Customer customer) {
        customer.contract.enabled = status;
      }
    }
  );
}
```

That's right—we can just take the `enabled` value as a parameter, which will then set the `enabled` member!

We've mostly purified our functions by extracting a `filter` function and a `foreach` function so that we don't need to rewrite our iteration functionality. We also changed our functions so that we're no longer directly accessing the `Customer.allCustomer` object; instead, we're passing it to our functions each time. This ensures that our functions' output will always be dependent on the input.

We still have a bit to do before our functions are completely pure; we need to get rid of the side effect that exists when we are changing our `Contact` variable.

Side Effects

Side effects are important: you can use them to persist data, display data, and even change fields on objects. Without side effects, most applications are completely useless. Here are a few examples of side effects:

- Printing to a screen
- Saving to a file/database
- Altering a field on an object

Side effects are not bad, they should just be used sparingly. They should be used only in certain situations because they go outside of the functional concepts. As we'll see in Chapter 7, statements allow us to implement side effects.

Back at XXY your boss has come to you again and said, "Boy, it's awesome that we can now set specific customers' contracts as disabled, but we really need to get information about those contracts after we've updated them." He essentially wants you to update `setContractForCustomer` to return a list of `Contract` objects you modified.

As stated before, assigning a field on an object passed in is technically a side effect. So, let's modify the `Contract` object's methods and return the `Contract` after updating the field. We're going to create some setters that actually return the object itself after it is modified! Let's look at the setters in Example 3-17.

Example 3-17. Customer class setters returning this

```java
public Customer setCustomerId(Integer customer_id) {
  this.id = customer_id;
  return this;
}

public Customer setName(String name) {
  this.name = name;
  return this;
}

public Customer setState(String state) {
  this.state = state;
  return this;
}

public Customer setDomain(String domain) {
  this.domain = domain;
  return this;
}

public Customer setEnabled(Boolean enabled) {
  this.enabled = enabled;
  return this;
}

public Customer setContract(Contract contract) {
  this.contract = contract;
  return this;
}
```

Let's also look at the setters that we're creating for our Contract class in Example 3-18. Again, we set the member variable and return our instance.

Example 3-18. Contract class setter returning this

```java
public Contract setBeginDate(Calendar begin_date) {
  this.begin_date = begin_date;
  return this;
}

public Contract setEndDate(Calendar end_date) {
  this.end_date = end_date;
  return this;
}

public Contract setEnabled(Boolean enabled) {
  this.enabled = enabled;
  return this;
}
```

Whereas we're trying to ensure that there are no functions that have side effects, we should no longer be using our `foreach` function. Instead, we'll be using a `map` or `collect` function. Let's write that really quickly so that we have it ready.

Our `map` function will take a list of anything and another function that will be used to transform each individual item it is passed. The code in Example 3-19 shows the new `map` function, which will exist inside our `Customer` class.

Example 3-19. map function from Customer.java

```
public static <A1,B> List<B> map(List<A1> inList, Function1<A1,B> func) {
  ArrayList<B> outList = new ArrayList<B>();
  for(A1 obj : inList) {
    outList.add(func.call(obj));
  }
  return outList;
}
```

Let's remember our `setContractForCustomer` function; we can refactor it to return the list of `Contracts` that were updated, as shown in Example 3-20. Notice how much simpler writing this code is? We can then use the return to print out each `Contract` that was updated.

Example 3-20. setContractForCustomer using map

```
public static List<Contract> setContractForCustomer(Integer customer_id, final
                                                     Boolean status) {
  return Customer.map(
    Customer.getCustomerById(Customer.allCustomers, customer_id),
    new Function1<Customer, Contract>() {
      public Contract call(Customer customer) {
        return customer.contract.setEnabled(status);
      }
    }
  );
}
```

We're now at the point where we need to abstract our `foreach`, `map`, and `filter` functions so that we're not just bound to our `Customer` object. Let's bring these out into their own singleton class, which we'll define in *FunctionalConcepts.java*, as shown in Example 3-21. Don't forget to update the references to these methods.

Example 3-21. FunctionalConcepts.java file

```
import java.util.ArrayList;
import java.util.List;

public class FunctionalConcepts {

  private FunctionalConcepts() {}
```

```
public static <A1,B> List<B> map(List<A1> inList, Function1<A1,B> func) {
  ArrayList<B> outList = new ArrayList<B>();
  for(A1 obj : inList) {
    outList.add(func.call(obj));
  }
  return outList;
}

public static <A> void foreach(ArrayList<A> inList, Foreach1<A> func) {
  for(A obj : inList) {
    func.call(obj);
  }
}

public static <A> ArrayList<A> filter(ArrayList<A> inList,
                                       Function1<A, Boolean> test) {
  ArrayList<A> outList = new ArrayList<A>();
  for(A obj : inList) {
    if(test.call(obj)) {
      outList.add(obj);
    }
  }
  return outList;
}

}
```

Now we just need to print the Contracts that changed, as shown in Example 3-22. Notice that we are implementing setContractForCustomer followed by a foreach on our returned list. We then create our Foreach function, which does the printing for us.

Example 3-22. foreach usage to print all modified contracts

```
FunctionalConcepts.foreach(
  Contract.setContractForCustomer(1, true),
  new Foreach1<Contract>() {
    public void call(Contract contract) {
      System.out.println(contract.toString());
    }
  }
);
```

We've ended up with a side effect again, so what are we going to do? As I said earlier, you can't entirely avoid side effects in your code. This being the case, we just need to wrap the side effect so that the output is always dependent on the input.

Conclusion

So far, we've discussed how to use higher-order functions to create more abstract functionality. I've also shown you how to take functions and make them pure, such that the entirety of the output is reliant on the parameter list.

It takes time and practice to really get the hang of refactoring into a functional style. My hope is that through this book you'll gain an understanding of how to make the changes.

How do you know when to make a function pure? Really, you want to make a function pure whenever possible; it makes the function much more testable and improves understandability from a troubleshooting perspective. However, sometimes you don't need to go to that extreme.

Let's look at Example 3-23, in which we'll refactor our `getField` method and instead of passing in the test function, we'll pass in a prefiltered list. That is a good purification, but let's not use the static `DisabledCustomers` object we created; instead, we'll create a new `Function1` with which to perform the filter.

Upon trying to purify the function, notice that we're now creating a new `Function1` object for every call to `getDisabledCustomerNames`. This isn't a huge deal, but remember that we have a lot of these `getDisabledCustomer*` functions, which means that we're going to duplicate a lot of these `Function1` objects. In this instance, we've taken purity too far, and instead we should've just used the `Customer.DisabledCustomer` object instead.

Example 3-23. Prefiltered lists with getDisabledCustomerNames

```
public static List<String> getDisabledCustomerNames() {
  return Customer.getField(
    FunctionalConcepts.filter(Customer.allCustomers,
                              new Function1<Customer,Boolean>() {
      public Boolean call(Customer customer) {
        return customer.enabled == false;
      }
    }),
    new Function1<Customer, String>() {
      public String call(Customer customer) { return customer.name; }
    }
  );
}

public static <B> List<B> getField(List<Customer> inList,
                                    Function1<Customer,B> func) {
  ArrayList<B> outList = new ArrayList<B>();
  for(Customer customer : inList) {
    outList.add(func.call(customer));
  }
```

```
    return outList;
}
```

Making the Switch to Groovy

Dynamically Typed Language

Groovy is a *dynamically typed language*, which means that you can create new types at runtime and the compiler won't warn you that you are passing incompatible types. In Groovy you overcome this by writing 100% unit tests in your code to ensure that you will not pass an invalid class to a function.

Your boss has started to see how useful functional programming is; he's been noticing how higher-order functions can reduce code duplication and sees the ease of testability that comes from having pure functions. He's decided that if you can keep the classes as they exist right now, you can go ahead and start converting over to another language.

You decide to convert to Groovy because it's fairly close to Java and allows people to write in Java if they are not fully comfortable with Groovy. Not only does Groovy allow us to keep the class definitions we already have, it also allows us to begin a transition to a fully functional language. As soon as we switch to Groovy, we will be able to get rid of our custom `FunctionalConcepts` class, as well as the `Function1` and `Foreach1` classes.

We will no longer need these classes, because Groovy includes helpful additions to the `List` interface such as `findAll` and `collect`, which are the same as `filter` and `map`, respectively. Let's see how we are going to refactor the update contract example. We'll begin by retrieving only the customer for the `id` we want, as shown in Example 3-24.

Example 3-24. getCustomerById in Groovy

```
def getCustomerById(Integer customerId) {
  Customer.allCustomers.findAll({ customer ->
    customer.id == customerId
  })
}
```

We now have a list of customers matching that `customer_id`; this list will be either empty or have one `Customer` in it, which, as we saw earlier in the chapter, is much safer to deal with than checking for nullity. Next, we need to take that list and update and send back the `Contract`, as in Example 3-25.

Example 3-25. Updating the contract field in Groovy

```
.collect({ customer ->
  customer.contract.enabled = false
  customer.contract
})
```

The last step is to print each of the contracts that we updated, as shown in Example 3-26.

Example 3-26. Printing all contracts in Groovy

```
.each({ contract ->
  println(contract)
})
```

Now, let's chain all of these calls together in Example 3-27.

Example 3-27. The setContractForCustomer method in Groovy

```
def setContractForCustomer(Integer customerId) {
  Customer.allCustomers.findAll({ customer ->
    customer.id == customerId
  }).collect({ customer ->
    customer.contract.setEnabled(false)
  }).each({ contract ->
    println contract
  })
}
```

What about all of those other methods from the *Customer.java* file? Let's go ahead and refactor our code into functional Groovy code. Let's do the getDisabledCustomer Names function first (see Example 3-28).

Example 3-28. getDisabledCustomerNames method in Groovy

```
public static List<String> getDisabledCustomerNames() {
  Customer.allCustomers.findAll({ customer ->
    customer.enabled == false
  }).collect({ cutomer ->
    cutomer.name
  })
}
```

Go ahead and refactor the *Customer.java* code into Groovy syntax. When you're done, check out the code in Example 3-29 to see how I refactored it.

Example 3-29. The Java-to-Groovy syntax

```
import java.util.ArrayList;
import java.util.List;

public class Customer {
```

```
static public ArrayList<Customer> allCustomers = new ArrayList<Customer>();
public Integer id = 0;
public String name = "";
public String address = "";
public String state = "";
public String primaryContact = "";
public String domain = "";
public Boolean enabled = true;
public Contract contract;

public Customer() {}


public Customer setCustomerId(Integer customer_id) {
  this.customer_id = customer_id;
  return this;
}

public Customer setName(String name) {
  this.name = name;
  return this;
}

public Customer setState(String state) {
  this.state = state;
  return this;
}

public Customer setDomain(String domain) {
  this.domain = domain;
  return this;
}

public Customer setEnabled(Boolean enabled) {
  this.enabled = enabled;
  return this;
}

public Customer setContract(Contract contract) {
  this.contract = contract;
  return this;
}

static def EnabledCustomer = { customer -> customer.enabled == true }
static def DisabledCustomer = { customer -> customer.enabled == false }

public static List<String> getDisabledCustomerNames() {
  Customer.allCustomers.findAll(DisabledCustomer).collect({cutomer ->
    cutomer.name
  })
}
```

```
public static List<String> getEnabledCustomerStates() {
  Customer.allCustomers.findAll(EnabledCustomer).collect({cutomer ->
    cutomer.state
  })
}

public static List<String> getEnabledCustomerDomains() {
  Customer.allCustomers.findAll(EnabledCustomer).collect({cutomer ->
    cutomer.domain
  })
}

public static List<String> getEnabledCustomerSomeoneEmail(String someone) {
  Customer.allCustomers.findAll(EnabledCustomer).collect({cutomer ->
    someone + "@" + cutomer.domain
  })
}

public static ArrayList<Customer> getCustomerById(ArrayList<Customer> inList,
                                                  final Integer customer_id) {
  inList.findAll({customer -> customer.customer_id == customer_id })
}
}
```

We can now get rid of the *FunctionalConcepts.java*, *Foreach1.java*, and *Function1.java* files because we're converting over to Groovy, which already have these built in.

Now that we've converted over, we'll be using Groovy from here on out. As I said before, Groovy is a fantastic transition language, since it makes it possible for you to bring in more functional concepts while keeping a syntax familiar to many Java programmers. You can continue writing in Java until everyone is more comfortable writing in a fully functional language. It also means that you can keep your libraries and current code without rewriting them.

CHAPTER 4

Immutable Variables

Immutable variables is a topic that gives everyone the shudders when they first get into it. Let's get the big question out of the way first: how can an application run if variables never change? This is a good question, so let's look at the following rules about immutability:

- Local variables do not change.
- Global variables can change only references.

Object variables, especially in Java, are references to the object itself. This means that changing the "reference" to which the variable points should be an atomic process. This is important because if we are going to update the variable, we will access it either pre- or post-update but never in an intermediate state. We'll discuss this a little later, but right now, let's look at mutability.

We're Getting Groovy Now
Remember from the preceding chapter that we're going to be writing in Groovy from this point on.

Mutability

When we think of variables, we normally think of mutable variables. After all, a variable is *variable*, which means that we should be able to store many different values in it and reuse it.

As we think of mutable variables, we realize that this is how we normally write code—with variables that inherently change over time. In Example 4-1, notice how f changes and is assigned two distinct values? This is how we normally deal with variables.

Example 4-1. Modifying a variable

```
def f = 10
f = f + f
```

So what happens when we have a variable that is passed to a function and we try to mutate that? Let's see in Example 4-2.

Example 4-2. Modifying a variable passed to a function

```
def f = "Foo"

def func(obj) {
  obj = "Bar"
}

println f
func(f)
println f
```

We can see from the output that we get two "Foo" printouts. This is correct because the reference that f contained, "Foo", was passed to func, and then we update the variable obj with a new reference to "Bar". But because there is no connection between obj and f, f remains unchanged and contains our original reference to "Foo".

This was probably *not* what the author intended, so he fixes it by using a mutable object *containing* the reference he wants to change. Let's see this in action in Example 4-3.

Example 4-3. Modifying a variable passed into a function

```
class Foo {
  String str
}

def f = new Foo(str: "Foo")

def func(Foo obj) {
  obj.str = "Bar"
}

println f.str
func(f)
println f.str
```

We can see that, although f didn't change, f.str did. This looks like it's a fairly standard mutation of an object, but let's think about this in another light. What if it were not clear that func was going to mutate f.str, and we now need to determine why f.str has changed over time? We'll need to debug to find out that func is indeed changing our variable.

Using code comments or setting something in the name of the function to indicate that you are mutating the object is one way to help answer the question "Why did this change?" Immutability gives us the confidence that our variables will not be changing and that our objects will be the same no matter to which function we send them.

Let's head back over to XXY. Your boss has come back with another request, this time a little more sane. He needs to send emails to the customers if the following conditions are met:

- The Customer is enabled.
- The Contract is enabled.
- The Contract has not expired.
- The Contact is still enabled.

The boss has indicated that this really shouldn't be a big deal because someone else already added a list of Contacts to the Customer class. The definition of a Contact is in the *Contact.java* file, shown in Example 4-4.

Example 4-4. Contact.java file

```java
public class Contact {

    public Integer contact_id = 0;
    public String firstName = "";
    public String lastName = "";
    public String email = "";
    public Boolean enabled = true;

    public Contact(Integer contact_id,
                   String firstName,
                   String lastName,
                   String email,
                   Boolean enabled) {
        this.contact_id = contact_id;
        this.firstName = firstName;
        this.lastName = lastName;
        this.email = email;
        this.enabled = enabled;
    }
}
```

The message template is as follows, where *<firstName>* and *<lastName>* are place-holders to be replaced by the user's name:

Hello *<firstName> <lastName>*,

We would like to let you know that a new product is available for you to try. Please feel free to give us a call at 1-800-555-1983 if you would like to see this product in action.

Sincerely, Your Friends at XXY

We're going to add the functionality into the Customer class. Let's think about this functionally. First, we will findAll Customer.allCustomer records where both the customer is enabled and the customer's contract is enabled. For each of those customers, we will then findAll contacts that are enabled. And finally, for each of those contacts, we will sendEmail. Let's go ahead and write the code in Groovy, as seen in Example 4-5.

Example 4-5. sendEnabledCustomersEmail method

```
public static void sendEnabledCustomersEmails(String msg) {
  Customer.allCustomers.findAll { customer ->
    customer.enabled && customer.contract.enabled
  }.each { customer ->
    customer.contacts.findAll { contact ->
      contact.enabled
    }.each { contact ->
      contact.sendEmail(msg)
    }
  }
}
```

I don't want to get too far into a battle about how best to handle sending emails, so let's assume that we've already written Contact.sendEmail, which takes a string, performs a replace for member variables, and then sends out the email. Let's get even more functional—we might need to do something else later for each enabled Contact. So, let's use a closure, as shown in Example 4-6.

Example 4-6. eachEnabledContact closure

```
public static void eachEnabledContact(Closure cls) {
  Customer.allCustomers.findAll { customer ->
    customer.enabled && customer.contract.enabled
  }.each { customer ->
    customer.contacts.each(cls)
  }
}
```

Now, we can call `Customer.eachEnabledContact({ contact -> contact.sendE mail(msg) })` and get our functionality. At this point, we have a nice set of functionality that we can call anytime we need to do something for all enabled contacts. For example, we might just want to create a list of all the enabled contacts.

Your boss has asked you to add functionality to change a `Contact`'s name and email, because people get married or have other life events requiring name changes. Now let's assume that our application is actually threaded (maybe it's a web server). If you don't see an issue, you're about to.

You just sat down to work, happy that you got the "change name and email" functionality done and rolled out. You get an email from your boss asking you to take a look at a new blocker bug: "Send email sometimes sends to an old email address." The support team includes the broken email in the bug as well.

from: XXY Product Trials <*trials@xxy.com*>

to: Jane Doe <*jdoe@company.com*>

subject: New Product Trial

Hello Jane Smith,

We would like to let you know that a new product is available for you to try. Please feel free to give us a call at 1-800-555-1983 if you would like to see this product in action.

Sincerely, Your Friends at XXY

In the bug, the support team says Jane just got married and her name changed from Jane Doe to Jane Smith. The thing they can't figure out is why the email went to Jane Doe <*jdoe@company.com*> but her name is referenced as Jane Smith in the body.

OK, before I break down the entire runtime, I'll try to explain this. User A updates the user's *last name* and *email* and clicks Save at the same time that another user clicks *Send email*. Because we have no synchronization, it's possible for the name to be updated but *not* the email when the email is actually created. Let's look at the simplified sequence of events in Table 4-1.

Table 4-1. Simplified user runtime

Step	User A	User B
1	Saves user name change	Clicks "Send email"
2	System updates last name	*Unscheduled*
3	*Unscheduled*	Sends email with inconsistent data
4	System updates email	*Unscheduled*

Concurrency means there is no guarantee that a shared variable will actually be in a specific state at any given time. How do you even reproduce concurrency bugs? How do you validate that you have actually fixed a concurrency bug?

We haven't even looked at a more likely scenario: what happens if we have functionality to remove a `Contact` or a `Customer`? Now we might be iterating over our list and remove an item from the list. Let's look at all of these issues in one fell swoop. There are two primary ways to fix our concurrency issue:

- Synchronize all access to the `Customer.allCustomers` object.
- Ensure that the `Customer.allCustomers` list and its members cannot be changed.

Our first option means that we must have a `synchronized` block for every possible access of the `Customer.allCustomers` object. Invariably someone will forget to do a synchronized access and break the entire paradigm.

Our second option is much better; anyone can write any accessor to the `Customer.allCustomers` variable without worrying about the list mutating. Of course, this means that we have to be able to generate new lists with updated members. This is the idea behind immutability.

Immutability

As we get deeper into immutability, think about database transactions. Database transactions are atomic, which means that the system is either in a pre-transaction or post-transaction state, never in a mid-transaction state.

This means that when a database transaction is committed, the new records are made available to new queries. Older queries are still using older data, which is fine because the functionality they were doing was predicated on the previous data.

Math Warning

I'm going to show that, if we have two good states, it's better to be in one or the other, but we cannot ever be in both. Let's begin by defining our function f(x,y). We also define that our two states (without the tick mark and with the tick mark) are not equal:

$$f(x, y) = \frac{x}{y}$$

$$31 * x + y \neq 31 * x' + y'$$

Let's create a set of our known two good states:

$$\beta = \{f(x, y), f(x', y')\}$$

So, this means that mixing the sets of parameters still works and still gives us a value; however, these are *not* values that exist in our set of good states.

$$f(x', y) \notin \beta$$

$$f(x, y') \notin \beta$$

So, we're going to think about variables as *placeholders* within a specific scope. If we think back to our email issue, then, we know that we can operate only in a *known good state* on both the list and the `Customer` and `Contact` records themselves.

Let's begin working on our fix by doing the simplest thing and making our `Customer.allCustomers` an immutable list. Remember, we're not making the variable immutable, we're making the thing the variable *contains* immutable. Let's see this in Example 4-7.

Example 4-7. Mutable allCustomers list that will contain immutable Customer objects

```
static public List<Customer> allCustomers = new ArrayList<Customer>();
```

That was simple enough, but now we have to deal with our `eachEnabledContact`, right? Actually, we don't have to do anything, because it was read-only functionality.

Let's continue our momentum and make all fields of the `Customer` object immutable. Again, this is fairly straightforward, as we make all fields `final` with one caveat: we must have a constructor that sets every field, as shown in Example 4-8.

Example 4-8. Immutable Customer object

```java
public final Integer customer_id = 0;
public final String name = "";
public final String state = "";
public final String domain = "";
public final Boolean enabled = true;
public final Contract contract = null;
public final List<Contact> contacts = new ArrayList<Contact>();

public Customer(Integer customer_id,
                String name,
                String state,
                String domain,
                Boolean enabled,
                Contract contract,
                List<Contact> contacts) {
    this.customer_id = customer_id;
    this.name = name;
    this.state = state;
    this.domain = domain;
    this.enabled = enabled;
    this.contract = contract;
    this.contacts = contacts;
}
```

Removing Setters

Because we're changing our fields to immutable, we must remove all
setters. If you think about it, having setters for *immutable* fields is a
fallacy in and of itself, because the fields can be set only when the
object is created.

Next, let's update our Contract class and make it immutable as well (Example 4-9). It
is important to understand that as we do this, we will be unable to run and test the
functionality until we've completed this refactor. Remember, our original code for updating a contract sets the field, which does not work with immutable variables.

Example 4-9. Immutable Contract class

```java
import java.util.List;
import java.util.Calendar;
import java.util.concurrent.ThreadPoolExecutor;
import java.util.concurrent.TimeUnit;
import java.util.concurrent.LinkedBlockingQueue;

public class Contract {

    public final Calendar begin_date;
    public final Calendar end_date;
    public final Boolean enabled = true;
```

```
public Contract(Calendar begin_date, Boolean enabled) {
  this.begin_date = begin_date;
  this.end_date = this.begin_date.getInstance();
  this.end_date.setTimeInMillis(this.begin_date.getTimeInMillis());
  this.end_date.add(Calendar.YEAR, 2);
  this.enabled = enabled;
}

}
```

Even though we know we need to update setContractForCustomerList, we're going to switch from a concurrent design for now. Instead, we'll create a new constructor, as shown in Example 4-10, so that we can create a new object with all members set.

Example 4-10. Constructor for the Contract class

```
public Contract(Calendar begin_date, Calendar end_date, Boolean enabled) {
  this.begin_date = begin_date;
  this.end_date = end_date;
  this.enabled = enabled;
}
```

Now, let's go ahead and update our setContractForCustomerList method so that we can get things working again. We'll want to *map* over our allCustomers list, updating customers that have specific ids. All of this is shown in Example 4-11.

Example 4-11. setContractForCustomerList with map

```
public static List<Customer> setContractForCustomerList(List<Integer> ids,
                                                        Boolean status) {
  Customer.allCustomers.collect { customer ->
    if(ids.indexOf(customer.customer_id) >= 0) {
      new Customer(
        customer.customer_id,
        customer.name,
        customer.state,
        customer.domain,
        customer.enabled,
        new Contract(
          customer.contract.begin_date,
          customer.contract.end_date,
          status
        ),
        customer.contacts
      )
    } else {
      customer
    }
  }
}
```

Some might think that this looks terrible, but it is a fantastic piece of code. We iterate over the list of objects, then check to see if the current `customer_id` is in our list of `id`s. If it is, we create a new customer, copying all the fields over *except* `Contract`. Instead, we create a new `Contract` with the specific status that was passed to us. This new customer is then used in place of the original customer record. If it is not in our list, we return the original customer.

Let's try to refactor this so that if we want to, we can change the `Contract` in *any* manner. We'll add a method to *Customer.java* called `updateContractForCustomerList`, which will do the same thing as Example 4-11, except now we execute a higher-order function on the contract itself. We will then expect that a contract will be returned. Let's look at the code in Example 4-12.

Example 4-12. updateContractForCustomerList function

```
public static List<Customer> updateContractForCustomerList(List<Integer> ids,
                                                           Closure cls) {
  Customer.allCustomers.collect { customer ->
    if(ids.indexOf(customer.customer_id) >= 0) {
      new Customer(
        customer.customer_id,
        customer.name,
        customer.state,
        customer.domain,
        customer.enabled,
        cls(customer.contract),
        customer.contacts
      )
    } else {
      customer
    }
  }
}
```

Now, we update our original `setContractForCustomerList` function in *Contract.java* to call into `Customer.updateContractForCustomerList`, as shown in Example 4-13. We are returning a `List` of `Customers`, so we are able to execute `Customer.allCustomers = Contract.setContractForCustomerList(...)`, which provides us with a constant, pristine list.

Example 4-13. setContractForCustomerList function, which references updateContract-ForCustomerList

```
public static List<Customer> setContractForCustomerList(List<Integer> ids,
                                                        Boolean status) {
  Customer.updateContractForCustomerList(ids, { contract ->
    new Contract(contract.begin_date, contract.end_date, status)
  })
}
```

Remember how I mentioned an update contact method earlier? This was the entire reason for our bug; let's go ahead and update that method so that we can fix the broken code, which is still trying to update objects.

In Example 4-14, we'll see our new `updateContact` method, which will *map* or *collect* all the `Customer` records.

Example 4-14. updateContactFor using an immutable list

```
public static List<Customer> updateContact(Integer customer_id,
                                           Integer contact_id,
                                           Closure cls) {
  Customer.allCustomers.collect { customer ->
    if(customer.customer_id == customer_id) {
      new Customer(
        customer.customer_id,
        customer.name,
        customer.state,
        customer.domain,
        customer.enabled,
        customer.contract,
        customer.contacts.collect { contact ->
          if(contact.contact_id == contact_id) {
            cls(contact)
          } else {
            contact
          }
        }
      )
    } else {
      customer
    }
  }
}
```

But wait: we're starting to repeat ourselves, so let's remember DRY and see what we can abstract. Take a few minutes to work on it yourself, and then check Example 4-15 to see what I did.

Example 4-15. Refactoring to abstract the looping methodology

```
public static List<Customer> updateCustomerByIdList(List<Integer> ids,
                                                    Closure cls) {
  Customer.allCustomers.collect { customer ->
    if(ids.indexOf(customer.customer_id) >= 0) {
      cls(customer)
    } else {
      customer
    }
  }
}
```

```
public static List<Customer> updateContact(Integer customer_id,
                                            Integer contact_id,
                                            Closure cls) {
  updateCustomerByIdList([customer_id], { customer ->
    new Customer(
      customer.customer_id,
      customer.name,
      customer.state,
      customer.domain,
      customer.enabled,
      customer.contract,
      customer.contacts.collect { contact ->
        if(contact.contact_id == contact_id) {
          cls(contact)
        } else {
          contact
        }
      }
    )
  })
}

public static List<Customer> updateContractForCustomerList(List<Integer> ids,
                                                           Closure cls) {
  updateCustomerByIdList(ids, { customer ->
    new Customer(
      customer.customer_id,
      customer.name,
      customer.state,
      customer.domain,
      customer.enabled,
      cls(customer.contract),
      customer.contacts
    )
  })
}
```

Conclusion

Most people believe that moving to immutable variables will increase the complexity of their code; however, it actually helps in many different ways. Tracking down bugs—because we know certain variables cannot change—becomes easier; we can better understand what might have been passed into and out of functions.

Immutability is a difficult technique to implement because you will most likely need to do large refactorings in order to accomplish it. Just look back at our conversion of the Customer object; we actually had to make changes to other classes and methods to support this. The key to implementing immutability is to start on your new classes and work backward during downtime to refactor your old code. Start with smaller classes that don't change much and then move on to your harder classes.

CHAPTER 5

Recursion

Immutable variables have an obvious flaw: we cannot change them. This means that it's more difficult to do things like changing a single element of a list, or implementing an if statement that sets a variable. Also, let's think about immutability in terms of applications. How can our applications run if data is never allowed to change? This is where we must use recursion.

Math Warning

Let's check out an example of a recursive function in mathematics. We can see that we have an *end case*: if x is less than or equal to 0. And we have the execution to do for every other case—this is our *summation*.

$$f(x) = \begin{cases} 0 & \text{if } x \leq 0 \\ x + f(x-1) & \text{if } x > 0 \end{cases}$$

Here we are just summing up each number that we pass in, but what if we used our first-class functions? Let's see what we could do.

$$f(x, c) = \begin{cases} 0 & \text{if } x \leq 0 \\ c(x) + f(x-1) & \text{if } x > 0 \end{cases}$$

Although it doesn't seem like much has changed, what we've effectively done is create the summation operation.

$$f(x, c) = \sum_{n=0}^{x} c(n)$$

Many people are afraid of recursion, mainly because they never learned how to write recursive functions effectively. People also assume that iterative algorithms are inherently better than recursive algorithms. Recursive algorithms are much simpler because they deal only with the input values. If we were to use a normal for loop in an iterative process, the algorithm would have to worry about the list as a whole. Example 5-1 shows a simple summation in a for loop.

Example 5-1. Summation using a for loop

```
def f(x) {
  int summation = 0
  for(int i = 1; i <= x; i++) { summation = summation + i }
  return summation
}
println f(10)
```

Let's rewrite this summation as a recursive function in Example 5-2.

Example 5-2. Summation using a recursive function

```
def f(x) {
  if(x <= 0) { return 0 } else { return x + f(x - 1) }
}
println f(10)
```

As in this case, a recursive algorithm is often much simpler to design, and I hope this chapter teaches you how to think recursively as you look at algorithms and puts you more at ease writing recursion.

As most software developers know, there is a limit on how *deep* recursion can go, or how many times a function can call into itself. Most of the time, this is bound by memory (remember, you're creating a new frame on the stack each time you make a function call), and in other languages there are limits in the compiler or interpreter. We'll discuss ways to get around this limitation, though unfortunately not for all languages.

An Introduction to Recursion

Let's think about another simple example to replicate the Filter function. We'll be writing this function in Groovy. Let's begin with a normal iterative loop style.

 You'll notice that I annotated the generic typing; although that's not required in Groovy, I don't want anyone to get lost.

```
def <T> List<T> Filter(List<T> list, Closure cls) {
  ArrayList<T> out = new ArrayList<T>()
  for(T obj : list) {
    if(cls(obj)) {
      out.add(obj)
    }
  }
  return out
}
```

As you can see, we create a mutable out list and then go through each element in our input list, adding it to our out list if cls(obj) returns true. As the final statement, we return out. Let's try to convert this iteration into recursion.

The first step is to check if the input list is empty; if it is, we'll return an empty list, as shown in Example 5-3. So far, we've protected ourselves from the *end case*, the most important part of a recursive function. This should always be your first step in writing a recursive function; if you miss this, you will end up with an infinite loop.

Example 5-3. Filter function with only the end case

```
def <T> List<T> Filter(List<T> list, Closure cls) {
  if(list.isEmpty()) {
    return []
  }
}
```

Lists, Heads, and Tails, Oh My!

There are generally two main parts of a list that everyone should understand: the *head* and the *tail*. Let's take, for example, a list of numbers from 1 to 5. The head is the element 1, whereas the tail is a list containing 2 through 5:

```
| 1 | 2 | 3 | 4 | 5 |
  ^     ^^^^^^^^^^^^
  |         |
 head      tail
```

After our if statement, we'll do our actual processing. We check when we pass list.head() to cls if that returns true. If it does, we'll create a new list containing the head; otherwise, we'll use an empty list (see Example 5-4).

Example 5-4. Filter function with the head portion of the list

```
def <T> List<T> Filter(List<T> list, Closure cls) {
  if(list.isEmpty()) {
    return []
  }
  List<T> out = cls(list.head()) ? [list.head()] : []
}
```

At this point, we know whether the current object belongs in our output list. But what about the rest of our list? That's easy: we'll just call back into `Filter` with the `tail()` of the list. We'll concatenate the returned list from `Filter` to our `out` list by using the `+` operator. Check out the code in Example 5-5.

Example 5-5. Basic Filter function using recursion

```
def <T> List<T> Filter(List<T> list, Closure cls) {
  if(list.isEmpty()) {
    return []
  }
  List<T> out = cls(list.head()) ? [list.head()] : []
  return out + Filter(list.tail(), cls)
}
```

But we can simplify this more. Let's complete the following steps and check out Example 5-6 once we're done:

1. Add an `else` statement to our `if` structure; this cleans up the *implicit* `else` that existed.

2. Get rid of the extraneous `out` variable by replacing it with the `ternary` statement.

Example 5-6. Simplified Filter function using recursion

```
def <T> List<T> Filter(List<T> list, Closure cls) {
  if(list.isEmpty()) {
    return []
  } else {
    return (cls(list.head()) ? [list.head()] : []) + Filter(list.tail(), cls)
  }
}
```

Nullity Is a Scary Thing

You'll notice that there was no check for `list` being `null`. This is actually intentional, because dealing with nullity is bad design. What would passing `null` to this function mean? Would it mean that your upstream function failed and you failed to handle it? If so, why should this function ignore nullity?

In my experience, `null` is a very dangerous construct that should be avoided at all costs. We'll see some alternatives to error handling later, but for now just know that we'll always pass around full objects.

The thing to notice about this algorithm is that in no instance is an object actually modified. Our objects are created and destroyed but are *never* mutated. Remember, immutability is an important part of functional programming.

Recursion

Sometimes the general `filter`- and `map`-style functions aren't going to help you. Instead, you will need to perform some operation to `reduce` the data from a set into a single piece of output.

XXY has been growing, and your boss has asked that you get a count of all enabled customers that have no enabled contacts. This is important because every customer should have at least one enabled contact. You start to write a simple function, falling back into an imperative style using iteration, as shown in Example 5-7.

Example 5-7. Function that counts a customer if she is enabled but has no enabled contacts

```
public static int countEnabledCustomersWithNoEnabledContacts(
                List<Customer> customers) {
  int total = 0
  for(Customer customer : customers) {
    if(customer.enabled) {
      if(customer.contacts.find({ contact -> contact.enabled}) == null) {
        total = total + 1
      }
    }
  }
  return total
}
```

Uh oh! Notice that we have a mutable variable. There is actually another solution using function chaining instead of recursion, as shown in Example 5-8.

Example 5-8. Function counting enabled customers, but no enabled contacts, using function chaining

```
public static int countEnabledCustomersWithNoEnabledContacts(
                List<Customer> customers) {
  return customers.findAll({ customer ->
    return customer.enabled
  }).findAll({ customer ->
    return (customer.contacts.find({ contact -> contact.enabled }) == null)
  }).size()
}
```

The problem here is that we're inherently traversing our list twice. Instead, let's go ahead and make this a single traversal by combining our `findAll` logic, as shown in Example 5-9.

Example 5-9. Function counting enabled customers, but no enabled contacts, in a single findAll

```
public static int countEnabledCustomersWithNoEnabledContacts(
                List<Customer> customers) {
  return customers.findAll({ customer ->
    return customer.enabled && (customer.contacts.find({ contact ->
                                    contact.enabled }) == null)
  }).size()
}
```

Of course, this is not a recursive function and relies on us creating a new list just to get the size() of the list. If this list were a couple thousand customers long, we'd be wasting time creating a new list that we're just going to throw away. Now, if we were going to just get the list and operate on that, it would be a different story, but here we're just concerned about the count.

Let's see how we can do this in a much less wasteful way. We're going to reduce over our list of customers into a count (see Example 5-10).

Example 5-10. Function counting enabled customers, but no enabled contacts, recursively

```
public static int countEnabledCustomersWithNoEnabledContacts(
                List<Customer> customers) {
  if(customers.isEmpty()) {
    return 0
  } else {
    int addition = (customers.head().enabled &&
      (customers.head().contacts.find({ contact ->
        contact.enabled
      }) == null)
    ) ? 1 : 0
    return addition + countEnabledCustomersWithNoEnabledContacts(customers.tail())
  }
}
```

Wow, there appears to be quite a bit going on here. There is, but what's amazing is that it's very simple logic and the overall statement is also really simple. Let's decompose this function. The first thing we'll do is define our *end case*, as shown in Example 5-11.

Example 5-11. Function counting enabled customers but no enabled contacts—end case

```
public static int countEnabledCustomersWithNoEnabledContacts(
                List<Customer> customers) {
  if(customers.isEmpty()) {
    return 0
  } else {
```

The next thing to do is define our logic *if the customer is enabled and has no enabled contacts*, which is shown in Example 5-12. We do this by saying, "if our logic is *true*, then we will add 1; otherwise, we add 0."

Example 5-12. Function counting enabled customers but no enabled contacts—base logic

```
int addition = (customers.head().enabled &&
  (customers.head().contacts.find({ contact ->
    contact.enabled
  }) == null)
) ? 1 : 0
```

Finally, we return our `addition` to our recursive call, as shown in Example 5-13.

Example 5-13. Function counting enabled customers but no enabled contacts—recursive call

```
    return addition + countEnabledCustomersWithNoEnabledContacts(customers.tail())
  }
}
```

The logic really isn't that bad. When we start looking at *statements* in Chapter 7, you will find that you really don't need to use the ternary operator. But for the time being, we'll proceed with the tools we have right now.

As I've said before, you can end up with some really bad issues if you have to recurse thousands of times. The main issue with recursing this many times is that you eventually run out of space on the stack. Remember, each function call pushes information back onto the stack. But, of course, there are instances for which we need to iterate thousands of times while keeping track of some state. This is where tail recursion comes in!

Tail Recursion

Tail recursion is very close to recursion, the difference being that there are no outstanding calls when you recurse. If you no longer need to keep the stack so that you can *unwind* the recursive calls, you no longer have an expanding stack.

Tail recursion happens when the last call of the function is the tail call and there are no outstanding operations to be done within the function when the return occurs. This is generally a compiler optimization, except in Groovy, which we will see shortly, for which you must use *trampolining*.

Let's look at our `Filter` example and see if we can convert this into a tail-recursive call. So, we know that in a tail call, the function cannot have outstanding processing when we go into a recurse. In Example 5-14, we'll add our end case and end parameter to return at the end.

Example 5-14. Filter function using tail recursion—only the end case

```
def <T> List<T> Filter(List<T> list, List<T> output, Closure cls) {
  if(list.isEmpty()) {
    return output
```

In our `else` statement, you'll notice that now we're *appending* to the output list instead of *prepending* to it (see Example 5-15). This is because we're building the list as we traverse it rather than as we unwind the stack.

Example 5-15. Filter function using tail recursion—the recursive call

```
  } else {
    return Filter(list.tail(), cls(list.head()) ? output + list.head() : output, cls)
  }
}
```

Let's put this all together and see what it looks like in Example 5-16.

Example 5-16. Filter function using tail recursion

```
def <T> List<T> Filter(List<T> list, List<T> output, Closure cls) {
  if(list.isEmpty()) {
    return output
  } else {
    return Filter(list.tail(), cls(list.head()) ? output + list.head() : output, cls)
  }
}
```

Refactoring Our countEnabledCustomersWithNoEnabledContacts Function

Your boss has come back saying that the `countEnabledCustomersWithNoEnabledCon tacts` function you wrote needs to handle a couple hundred thousand customers. You've known from the beginning that the function you wrote would fail if you go too deep into the recursion. But, there is a way to fix our recursive call, so let's do so.

Let's begin with the end case again. In Example 5-17, we know that our last step should be returning the sum. We will then add sum as a parameter to our function to be returned in the end case.

Example 5-17. Base case of tail-recursive countEnabledCustomersWithNoEnabledContacts

```
public static int countEnabledCustomersWithNoEnabledContacts(
                List<Customer> customers,
                int sum) {
  if(customers.isEmpty()) {
    return sum
  } else {
```

Again, we have the same logic to determine whether we're adding anything (see Example 5-18.

Example 5-18. Base logic of tail-recursive countEnabledCustomersWithNoEnabled-Contacts

```
int addition = (customers.head().enabled &&
  (customers.head().contacts.find({ contact ->
    contact.enabled
  }) == null)
) ? 1 : 0
```

Finally, we recurse into our function, adding the `addition` to our `sum`, which we then pass forward, as in Example 5-19. This passing forward, and the fact that we have nothing waiting on the return of that function, is what makes this function tail-recursive. As soon as we hit the end case, the value returned from the end case will be the same value that is returned from the entrance into the recursive call itself.

Example 5-19. Return of tail-recursive countEnabledCustomersWithNoEnabledContacts

```
    return countEnabledCustomersWithNoEnabledContacts(customers.tail(),
                                              sum + addition)
  }
}
```

As you can see, we're still not mutating any objects, and we're compiling our summation as we recurse instead of having to unwind all of our function calls. Let's see this all put together in Example 5-20.

Example 5-20. Tail-recursive countEnabledCustomersWithNoEnabledContacts

```
public static int countEnabledCustomersWithNoEnabledContacts(
                List<Customer> customers,
                int sum) {
  if(customers.isEmpty()) {
    return sum
  } else {
    int addition = (customers.head().enabled &&
      (customers.head().contacts.find({ contact ->
        contact.enabled
      }) == null)
    ) ? 1 : 0
    return countEnabledCustomersWithNoEnabledContacts(customers.tail(),
                                              sum + addition)
  }
}
```

Awesome! Now we have a tail-recursive call. Unfortunately, Groovy does not actually *do* a tail-recursive optimization. But we have one small trick up our sleeves. We need to turn this into a lambda and use the `trampoline()` call on it. Our code in Example 5-21 shows this refactor.

So how does trampolining work? It's pretty simple: the `trampoline()` call causes the function to be wrapped in a `TrampolineClosure`. When we execute the `Trampoline Closure`—for example, calling `countEnabledCustomersWithNoEnabledContacts(Customer.allCustomers, 0)`—it will then execute the function itself. If the execution returns a `TrampolineClosure`, it will run the new `TrampolineClosure` function. It will continue to do this until it gets something back that is *not* a `TrampolineClosure`.

Example 5-21. Function counting enabled customers, but no enabled contacts, tail recursively, using trampolining

```
def countEnabledCustomersWithNoEnabledContacts = null
countEnabledCustomersWithNoEnabledContacts = { List<Customer> customers, int sum ->
  if(customers.isEmpty()) {
    return sum
  } else {
    int addition = (customers.head().enabled &&
      (customers.head().contacts.find({ contact ->
        contact.enabled
      }) == null)
    ) ? 1 : 0
    return countEnabledCustomersWithNoEnabledContacts.trampoline(customers.tail(),
                                                    sum + addition)
  }
}.trampoline()
```

Conclusion

In this chapter, we created a new function called `countEnabledCustomersWithNoEnabledContacts` as a general recursive function, and then refactored it into a tail-recursive function call. Notice that the logic is much simpler than using an entire `if` structure. Instead, we can just look at the first element from our list, the head, and determine whether we want to count it.

Many people shy away from recursion because of depth concerns and a perceived "performance issue." That is valid when you start looking at extremely large lists and how many function calls are actually being done. But let's look at our email example from Chapter 4.

Let's assume that we have five threads and a list of *n* size, and we are going to synchronize access to the list (allowing mutable objects). Let's assume that one of those threads needs to update something in the list, meaning that it's locking the list and giving a runtime of O(n). That's not too bad, but what about the other four threads? They are now *blocked* for O(n) and will eventually have their own runtime of O(n). This brings the runtime to O(2n).

Now, let's look at this same example but instead using immutability and recursion. Let's assume that our update thread has a runtime of O(n), and our other threads also have their own runtime of O(n). Notice, though, that the other threads do not need to *wait* for writing to finish before they are able to access that list. This brings the runtime to O(n). Let's remember that in time complexity O(2n) can be simplified to O(n), which means that both an iterative and a recursive runtime should be fairly similar when we're looking at concurrent processing.

Tail recursion solves our depth issues, but we have some challenges with syntax. As we saw with Groovy, we had to define a variable and then call .trampoline() on the closure that we were assigning to the variable. We can then use the trampoline() function call in order to return a function to execute.

Introducing Scala

Let's revisit our countEnabledCustomersWithNoEnabledContacts method, but this time let's look at it in Scala (shown in Example 5-22) and see how it's different. As we'll see in the next few chapters, languages like Scala are more expressive, making recursion much more readable and understandable.

Example 5-22. Function counting enabled customers, but no enabled contacts, tail recursively in Scala

```
def countEnabledCustomersWithNoEnabledContacts(customers : List[Customer],
    sum : Int) : Int = {
  if(customers.isEmpty) {
    return sum
  } else {
    val addition : Int = if(customers.head().enabled &&
                        (customers.head().contacts.count(contact =>
                          contact.enabled)) > 0) { 1 } else { 0 }
    return countEnabledCustomersWithNoEnabledContacts(customers.tail,
                                          sum + addition)
  }
}
```

Scala Syntax

There are a few things to note here about the Scala syntax in Example 5-22:

- Functions are denoted using the `def` keyword.
- Types are always listed *after* the definition and are separated with the `:` operator.
- The `isEmpty` method call does not require us to use an empty set of parentheses (because we treat it more like a member than a method).
- Instead of using the *ternary* operator, we can use a full `if` statement to achieve the same effect.

The biggest difference is that we no longer have to call `trampoline()`; instead, we just make our recursive call. As a double check, we can actually include the `@tailrec` annotation on the method, which forces the compiler to make sure this method *is* tail-recursive.

The other difference is that we have the `if` statement, which has a `1` or a `0` inside the `if`/`else` structure setting the `addition` variable. This is equivalent to the ternary operator.

In the coming chapters, we'll see more examples of this, specifically when we start talking about statements.

CHAPTER 6
Strict and Nonstrict Evaluations

Evaluations are the execution of a statement, usually the execution and setting of a variable. So what exactly does it mean to have a *strict* versus a *nonstrict* evaluation? Generally speaking, we as developers use strict evaluations. This means that the statement is immediately evaluated and assigned to the variable as soon as the variable is defined.

This obviously means that with nonstrict evaluations we don't assign the variable where it is defined. This is also known as a "lazy" variable; the variable isn't actually assigned until the first time it is used. This is really useful when we have variables that may not be used in a specific situation. Let's look at a mathematical example.

Math Warning
Let's assume that we have three functions: a(x), b(x), and f(x).

$$f(x) = a(x) / b(x)$$

If we look at this equation, we know to evaluate b(x) first because if it equals 0, there is no point in evaluating a(x) given that the entire equation fails. Our *lazy* value is a(x), and this is the point of a lazy variable.

When thinking of lazy variables, we tend to also think of mutable variables, because we think of the variable being defined and eventually being set. We normally think about the Java example in Example 6-1. However, with nonstrict evaluation, we maintain immutability; the variable is assigned or evaluated only on the first reference. This means that before the variable is used, it doesn't exist; and as soon as it's referenced, the variable becomes defined.

Example 6-1. A lazy variable in Java

```java
public static double f(int x) {
        int brtn = b(x);
        if(brtn == 0) {
                throw new IllegalArgumentException("Input gave a 0 value from b(x)");
        }
        return a(x) / brtn;
}
```

Your boss at XXY has asked that you create a new function that can get a list of enabled `Contacts` for all enabled `Customers`. Let's start with the simplest implementation by using a method. The method will be called `enabledContacts()`, and we'll add it to the `Customer`. We see this implementation in Example 6-2.

Example 6-2. All enabled contacts method in Customer.java

```java
public List<Contact> enabledContacts() {
    contacts.findAll { contact -> contact.enabled }
}
```

Well, that was pretty easy, but what happens if we call this multiple times? That's an easy fix: let's just make this into a member variable instead of a method.

Strict Evaluation

So, *strict evaluation* means that we will create and evaluate the setting of the variable at the time we define it. This is how we normally think of variables, so let's go ahead and initialize our `enabledContacts` member during the creation of the `Customer` object, as shown in Example 6-3.

Example 6-3. All enabled contacts member being set in constructor

```java
this.enabledContacts = contacts.findAll { contact -> contact.enabled }
```

Awesome—now we have our `enabledContacts` member, which can be accessed as many times as we want and we don't have to worry about rerunning the `findAll`. So let's go ahead and write our code to actually obtain all enabled `Contacts` for all enabled `Customers`. We'll need to add a quick function call to `flatten()` because our `enabledContacts` is a list, and we're collecting a list of those lists to have a result of `List<List<Contact>>`. The call to `flatten()` will collapse all of the inner lists together and return a `List<Contact>` (Example 6-4).

Example 6-4. Iterate over all customers and get their enabledContacts

```
Customer.allCustomers.findAll { customer ->
  customer.enabled
}.collect { customer ->
  customer.enabledContacts()
}.flatten()
```

Uh oh, our boss has come back saying that the application is taking *forever* to start up and run. Since we're using *static evaluation*, we're actually creating our enabledCon tacts list even if the Customer was disabled; so how can we skip *evaluating* the variable if we don't need it? Lazy evaluation allows us to *define* the variable but not evaluate its value until the first time it is referenced.

Nonstrict (Lazy) Evaluation

So let's start by following the normal imperative method most people would use to accomplish this. We'll create the member as private and then add a getter method. We'll then synchronize the method and check to see if the object is initialized, creating it if not, and then return that (Example 6-5).

Example 6-5. All enabled contacts method with deduplication in Customer.java

```
private List<Contact> enabledContacts = null

public synchronized List<Contact> getEnabledContacts() {
      if(this.enabledContacts == null) {
              this.enabledContacts = this.contacts.findAll { contact ->
                      contact.enabled
              }
      }
      return this.enabledContacts
}
```

Obviously this works, but it's really undesirable because now we have a completely different methodology to access the enabledContacts member. We're actually going to be calling a method rather than doing a simple member access. Good thing we're using Groovy and we get the @Lazy annotation!

Before we start throwing around the @Lazy annotation, let's actually play around with lazy variables in separate scripts. We'll create a simple class TestClass, which will have an array of numbers from 1 to 6, and another that contains only the odd numbers, as shown in Example 6-6.

Running Examples

For the rest of the examples in this chapter, these are all scripts and there is no need for compilation.

Groovy examples

> Copy the code into a file and run "groovy filename.groovy".

Scala example

> Copy the code into a file and run "scala filename.scala".

Example 6-6. TestClass with nonlazy member

```
class TestClass {

  def all = [1,2,3,4,5,6]
  def odd = all.findAll { num -> num%2 == 1 }

}

println(new TestClass().odd)
```

So we obviously know that the member odd gets initialized as soon as we call `new Temp Class()`. But let's verify this by modifying the code a bit, as in Example 6-7.

Example 6-7. TestClass with nonlazy member and print statements

```
class TestClass {

  def all = [1,2,3,4,5,6]
  def odd = all.findAll { num -> println("Foo"); num%2 == 1; }

}

def tc = new TestClass()

println("Bar")

println(tc.odd)
```

As assumed, we see a bunch of "Foo" statements get printed followed by a "Bar", and finally the array itself. But we can change this functionality by adding the @Lazy annotation to the odd member, as shown in Example 6-8.

Example 6-8. TestClass with lazy member and print statements

```
class TestClass {

  def all = [1,2,3,4,5,6]
  @Lazy def odd = all.findAll { num -> println("Foo"); num%2 == 1; }

}
```

```
def tc = new TestClass()

println("Bar")

println(tc.odd)
```

As we can see, we have the "Bar" printed out followed by a bunch of "Foo" statements and finally the array. Notice that the odd member doesn't actually get evaluated until it's referenced. Now, this has a really nasty side effect: if we were to change all before we called odd, then when we *do* call odd we're going to be getting the *new* evaluation based on the *new* value of all. This is shown in Example 6-9.

Example 6-9. TestClass with lazy member; we change the all variable before referencing odd

```
class TestClass {

  def all = [1,2,3,4,5,6]
  @Lazy def odd = all.findAll { num -> num%2 == 1 }

}

def tc = new TestClass()

tc.all = [1,2,3]

println(tc.odd)
```

The output here is the list of odd numbers but only between 1 and 3 (because we referenced odd after we had changed the all variable). So what happens if we reference odd before we change the all variable? Does this mean that the variable odd would be set and would no longer be updated? Let's see this in Example 6-10.

Example 6-10. TestClass with lazy member; we change the all variable reference after referencing odd

```
class TestClass {

  def all = [1,2,3,4,5,6]
  @Lazy def odd = all.findAll { num -> num%2 == 1 }

}

def tc = new TestClass()

println(tc.odd)

tc.all = [1,2,3]

println(tc.odd)
```

We see two lists printed out that are exactly the same; they are of odd numbers from 1 to 5. Wait—we changed all, which should mean that the second list we printed out should've been odd numbers, but only from 1 to 3. Ah, but as we said before: the laziness of the odd variable means that the evaluation only occurs once. This means on the first reference of odd, it will be set and will not be reevaluated.

So now, let's make use of the @Lazy annotation on our enabledContacts variable, as in Example 6-11.

Being Lazy Has Its Own Quirks

In Groovy, when we use the @Lazy annotation, the Groovy compiler generates a getter for the member, which does a lazy generation of the member. This means that it will create it on the first access if it doesn't already exist, but if it does will reuse it. This works until you try to use the final modifier.

Groovy will then pass the final modifier directly to Java, and you will end up trying to modify a final variable due to the way @Lazy works.

Example 6-11. All enabled contacts as lazy member in Customer.java

```
@Lazy public volatile List<Contact> enabledContacts = contacts.findAll { contact ->
  contact.enabled
}
```

Concurrency Notice

In Groovy, you will need to add the volatile keyword when using @Lazy; otherwise, this code gets converted into non–thread-safe code.

In Example 6-12, let's look at a lazy variable definition in Scala for comparison.

Example 6-12. All enabled contacts as lazy member in Scala

```
lazy val enabledContacts = contacts.filter { contact ->
  contact.enabled
}
```

Notice that lazy becomes a modifier. For those not familiar with Scala, defining a variable is done with val or var, meaning an immutable or mutable variable respectively. Finally, we filter our contacts. Notice that the big difference between Scala and Groovy within the anonymous function syntax is switching from -> to =>, which separates our parameters from the body.

Laziness Can Create Problems

Sometimes creating lazy variables can cause problems; for example, let's say that you have a variable that a large number of threads rely on. If you use a lazy variable, this means that all the threads will block until the variable has been computed.

Let's see an example where doing lazy variables might be worse than if we just took the time to compute it in the beginning. We're going to step away from XXY and look at a simple example. Let's assume that we have a `Customer` container, as shown in Example 6-13.

Example 6-13. Problem with laziness shown in Groovy

```groovy
class Customer {
  final Integer id
  final Boolean enabled
  public Customer(id, enabled) { this.id = id; this.enabled = enabled; }
}

class CustomerContainer {
  public List<Customer> customers = []
  @Lazy public volatile List<Customer> onlyEnabled = {
    customers.findAll { customer ->
      customer.enabled
    }
  }()
  public CustomerContainer() { this([]) }
  public CustomerContainer(customers) { this.customers = customers }
  def addCustomer(c) {
    new CustomerContainer(customers.plus(customers.size(), [c]))
  }
  def removeCustomer(c) {
    new CustomerContainer(customers.findAll { customer -> customer.id != c.id })
  }
}

def cc = new CustomerContainer()
cc = cc.addCustomer(new Customer(1, true))
cc = cc.addCustomer(new Customer(2, false))
println(cc.customers)
```

So now we have a container that we can keep updating in a thread-safe manner. Notice, though, that we have our `onlyEnabled` as a `@Lazy` variable. The unfortunate part here is that the runtime slows down if we are constantly changing the container and we have a multitude of threads. Each time the container refreshes, all threads will block on access to the `onlyEnabled` field the first time it is accessed. Let's try to fix this in Example 6-14.

Example 6-14. Problem with laziness in Groovy, fixed

```
class Customer {
  final Integer id
  final Boolean enabled
  public Customer(id, enabled) { this.id = id; this.enabled = enabled; }
}

class CustomerContainer {
  public List<Customer> customers = []
  public List<Customer> onlyEnabled = []
  public CustomerContainer() { this([]) }
  public CustomerContainer(customers) {
    this.customers = customers
    this.onlyEnabled = customers.findAll { customer -> customer.enabled }
  }
  def addCustomer(c) {
    new CustomerContainer(customers.plus(customers.size(), [c]))
  }
  def removeCustomer(c) {
    new CustomerContainer(customers.findAll { customer -> customer.id != c.id })
  }
}

def cc = new CustomerContainer()
cc = cc.addCustomer(new Customer(1, true))
cc = cc.addCustomer(new Customer(2, false))
println(cc.customers)
```

By removing the @Lazy annotation, the *only* thread responsible for adding/removing customers will be the one that blocks and takes the time to populate our list. Now, the rest of our threads can continue to process requests without blocking on the first call to onlyEnabled.

But where *would* a good place to use laziness be in this example? Let's assume that there is a revenue number tied to every customer which is based on their contracts. In example Example 6-15 there is a revenue variable in our Customer class, but we don't always need to evaluate that variable, which is why we've used a @Lazy variable.

Example 6-15. Lazy calculation of revenue variable in Groovy

```
class Customer {
  final Integer id
  final Boolean enabled
  final List<Double> contracts
  @Lazy volatile Double revenue = calculateRevenue(this.contracts)
  static def calculateRevenue(contracts) {
    Double sum = 0.0
    for(Double contract : contracts) {
      sum += contract
    }
```

```
      sum
  }
  public Customer(id, enabled, contracts) {
    this.id = id
    this.enabled = enabled
    this.contracts = contracts
  }
}

class CustomerContainer {
  public List<Customer> customers = []
  public List<Customer> onlyEnabled = []
  public CustomerContainer() { this([]) }
  public CustomerContainer(customers) {
    this.customers = customers
    this.onlyEnabled = customers.findAll { customer -> customer.enabled }
  }
  def addCustomer(c) {
    new CustomerContainer(customers.plus(customers.size(), [c]))
  }
  def removeCustomer(c) {
    new CustomerContainer(customers.findAll { customer -> customer.id != c.id })
  }
}

def cc = new CustomerContainer()
cc = cc.addCustomer(new Customer(1, true, [100.0, 200.0, 300.0]))
cc = cc.addCustomer(new Customer(2, false, [100.0, 150.0, 500.0]))
println(cc.customers)
Double sum = 0.0
for(Customer customer : cc.onlyEnabled) {
  sum += customer.revenue
}
println("Enabled Revenue: ${sum}")
```

Since we're going to be diving into Scala due to its increased focus on functional programming, in Example 6-16, the exact same functionality shown in Example 6-15 is rewritten in Scala. This is for a direct comparison and will give you a good idea of the syntax and some basics of Scala.

Example 6-16. Scala representation of Example 6-15

```
class Customer(val id : Integer,
               val enabled : Boolean,
               val contracts : List[Double]) {

  lazy val revenue : Double = calculateRevenue(this.contracts)

  def calculateRevenue(contracts : List[Double]) : Double = {
    var sum : Double = 0.0
    for(contract <- contracts) {
      sum += contract
```

```
    }
    sum
  }
}

class CustomerContainer(val customers : List[Customer] = List()) {

  val onlyEnabled = customers.filter { customer => customer.enabled }

  def addCustomer(c : Customer) : CustomerContainer = {
    new CustomerContainer(customers ::: List(c))
  }

  def removeCustomer(c : Customer) : CustomerContainer = {
    new CustomerContainer(customers.filter { customer => customer.id != c.id })
  }

}

var cc = new CustomerContainer()

cc = cc.addCustomer(new Customer(1, true, List(100.0, 200.0, 300.0)))
cc = cc.addCustomer(new Customer(2, false, List(100.0, 150.0, 500.0)))

println(cc.customers)

var sum : Double = 0.0
for(customer <- cc.onlyEnabled) {
  sum += customer.revenue
}

println(s"Enabled Revenue: ${sum}")
```

Conclusion

Lazy evaluations have allowed us to speed up the runtime of our application, since we only need to build our `enabledCustomers` when we need it. We've also learned that there are times we need to be careful, as we may end up blocking all of our threads from working while the lazy variable is evaluated.

There are obvious pros and cons to utilizing strict and nonstrict (lazy) evaluations; learning when and where to use them is important in producing good functional code. It allows us to describe variables that we don't necessarily want to waste processing time on if we don't need to.

Many of you may have already seen some of these concepts in Object-Relational Mappers (ORMs) such as Hibernate with a lazy fetch. Generally you use it in relationships between objects, so that you don't load hundreds of relationships unless you absolutely need to.

Now think about when you may not want to. For example, you might have a `Contact` object as well as a linkage to its friends which were also `Contacts`. Maybe you need that every time the user logs in; if so, a lazy variable is not going to help you.

Generally speaking, strict evaluation is important when you have frequently accessed members of an object—especially if they exist in a multithreaded environment and are being used by all threads. On the other hand, if you have variables that are referenced infrequently or are extremely expensive to compute, it's more useful to evaluate them only if absolutely necessary.

CHAPTER 7

Statements

When we think of a *statement*, we think of something like `Integer x = 1;` or `val x = 1` where we are setting a variable. Technically, that line evaluates to nothing, but what if we had already defined a variable, and we were setting it later—something like `x = 1`? Some people already know that in C and Java, this statement actually returns 1, as shown in Example 7-1.

Example 7-1. A simple assignment statement

```
public class Test {

  public static void main(String[] args) {
    Integer x = 0;
    System.out.println("X is " + (x = 1).toString());
  }

}
```

Statements in functional programming introduce the idea that every line of code should have a return value. Imperative languages such as Java incorporate the concept of the *ternary* operator. This gives you an `if/else` structure that evaluates to a value. Example 7-2 shows a simple usage of the ternary operator.

Example 7-2. A simple ternary statement

```
public class Test {

  public static void main(String[] args) {
    Integer x = 1;
    System.out.println("X is: " + ((x > 0) ? "positive" : "negative"));
  }

}
```

But if we're able to make more use of statements, we can actually reduce the number of variables we have. If we reduce the number of variables that we have, we reduce the ability to mutate them and thus increase our ability to perform concurrent processes *and* become more functional!

Taking the Plunge

Your boss is very happy with what you've been doing over at XXY. He's actually impressed with functional programming and wants you to convert from a partially functional language to a fully functional one. This shouldn't be difficult, because we've already become quite functional over the last few chapters.

We're going to pick a language that still runs on the Java Virtual Machine (JVM) so that we're not introducing a new technology such as the LISP runtime or the Erlang runtime. We could also pick a language such as Clojure or Erjang, but for the purpose of this book we're using Scala, which is similar to the Java syntax and should not require a huge learning curve.

Simple Statements

We'll be rewriting each of our classes, so let's begin with the easiest of the files: the Contact class. You'll remember the existing file, shown in Example 7-3.

Example 7-3. Contact.java file

```
public class Contact {

        public final Integer contact_id = 0;
        public final String firstName = "";
        public final String lastName = "";
        public final String email = "";
        public final Boolean enabled = true;

        public Contact(Integer contact_id,
                    String firstName,
                    String lastName,
                    String email,
                    Boolean enabled) {
            this.contact_id = contact_id;
            this.firstName = firstName;
            this.lastName = lastName;
            this.email = email;
            this.enabled = enabled;
        }

        public static List<Customer> setNameAndEmailForContactAndCustomer(
                    Integer customer_id,
                    Integer contact_id,
```

```
                    String name,
                    String email) {
        Customer.updateContactForCustomerContact(
                customer_id,
                contact_id,
                { contact ->
                        new Contact(
                                contact.contact_id,
                                contact.firstName,
                                name,
                                email,
                                contact.enabled
                        )
                }
        )
    }

    public void sendEmail() {
            println("Sending Email")
    }

}
```

We'll refactor this into its Scala equivalent, as shown in Example 7-4. In the Scala example, notice that we define our instance variables in a set of parentheses next to the class name. We also have an *object* and a *class*; *static* methods and members exist inside the *object* rather than the *class* definition. Types are also defined *after* the variable rather than *before* it.

Example 7-4. Contact.scala file

```
object Contact {

    def setNameAndEmailForContactAndCustomer(
        customer_id : Integer,
            contact_id : Integer,
            name : String,
            email : String) : List[Customer] = {
    Customer.updateContactForCustomerContact(
        customer_id,
        contact_id,
        { contact =>
                new Contact(
          contact.contact_id,
          contact.firstName,
          name,
          email,
          contact.enabled
        )
      }
    )
  }
}
```

```
}

class Contact(val contact_id : Integer,
              val firstName : String,
              val lastName : String,
              val email : String,
              val enabled : Boolean) {

  def sendEmail() = {
      println("Sending Email")
  }

}
```

 Although there are lots of lines added for readability in this book, including empty lines and method definitions split onto multiple lines, the number of lines goes from 19 to 9. This results from how we define members in Java and how we set them via the constructor.

Block Statements

The next class we're going to tackle is the Contact class. This is a little more difficult because we were using a Java Calendar object, which is not a very functional construct. Let's take a look at the original file in Example 7-5.

Example 7-5. Contract.java file

```
import java.util.List;
import java.util.Calendar;

public class Contract {

        public final Calendar begin_date;
        public final Calendar end_date;
        public final Boolean enabled = true;

        public Contract(Calendar begin_date, Calendar end_date, Boolean enabled) {
                this.begin_date = begin_date;
                this.end_date = end_date;
                this.enabled = enabled;
        }

        public Contract(Calendar begin_date, Boolean enabled) {
                this.begin_date = begin_date;
                this.end_date = this.begin_date.getInstance();
                this.end_date.setTimeInMillis(this.begin_date.getTimeInMillis());
                this.end_date.add(Calendar.YEAR, 2);
                this.enabled = enabled;
        }
```

```
    public static List<Customer> setContractForCustomerList(
            List<Integer> ids,
            Boolean status) {
        Customer.updateContractForCustomerList(ids) { contract ->
            new Contract(contract.begin_date, contract.end_date, status)
        }
    }
}
```

We'll go ahead and convert the class over, as shown in Example 7-6. Let's first look at the List[Integer], which is how Scala denotes generic typing. We'll also see a very interesting syntax with def this(begin_date : Calendar, enabled : Boolean), which is how we define an alternate constructor. We can also see a line that just has a c; this is actually valid because the line is treated as a *statement*. This line is then treated as the return value of that block of code.

What is most interesting about this syntax is the call to this, in which we pass what appears to be a function where the end_date variable should be passed. Why is the compiler not complaining that a Calendar instance is expected, not a method that returns a Calendar instance?

Example 7-6. Contract.scala file

```
import java.util.Calendar

object Contract {

  def setContractForCustomerList(ids : List[Integer],
                          status : Boolean) : List[Customer] = {
      Customer.updateContractForCustomerList(ids, { contract =>
        new Contract(contract.begin_date, contract.end_date, status)
    })
  }

}

class Contract(val begin_date : Calendar,
              val end_date : Calendar,
              val enabled : Boolean) {

  def this(begin_date : Calendar, enabled : Boolean) = this(begin_date, {
    val c = Calendar.getInstance()
    c.setTimeInMillis(begin_date.getTimeInMillis)
    c.add(Calendar.YEAR, 2)
    c
  }, enabled)

}
```

The compiler infers that you are not passing a method, but instead wanting to *evaluate* the brackets {. . .}. So when the alternate constructor is called, we will call into the actual constructor, and the brackets {. . .} will be evaluated to come up with the end_date Calendar object. Alternate constructors are much like how Java allows you to overload constructors to take different arguments.

The code block shown in Example 7-7 is very simple; it creates a Calendar object, setting the time in milliseconds based on our begin_date object (reminiscent of a closure). It then adds two years to the time in order to create a time that is two years from the beginning of the contract. Finally, it returns our newly created c object containing two years from begin_date.

This statement makes it possible for us to step outside the normal functional paradigm, in which every line should be a statement that can then be directed into another function or used directly. You can think of this as a compound statement: you have multiple statements that must be evaluated in order to come up with an overall statement that is actually used.

Example 7-7. Code block of end_date

```
{
  val c = Calendar.getInstance()
  c.setTimeInMillis(begin_date.getTimeInMillis)
  c.add(Calendar.YEAR, 2)
  c
}
```

The interesting thing about this block of code is that it shows that, quite literally, everything is a statement. Think about this: the last line, c, is a statement because it returns the variable c. And the entire code block is a statement itself; when evaluated, it executes the lines of code in sequence and returns the new c value we defined.

Everything Is a Statement

Finally, we're going to convert our Customer class, which shouldn't be too hard; let's look at the original Java file shown in Example 7-8.

Example 7-8. Customer.java file

```
import java.util.ArrayList;
import java.util.List;
import java.util.Calendar;

public class Customer {

    static public List<Customer> allCustomers = new ArrayList<Customer>();
    public final Integer id = 0;
    public final String name = "";
```

```
public final String state = "";
public final String domain = "";
public final Boolean enabled = true;
public final Contract contract = null;
public final List<Contact> contacts = new ArrayList<Contact>();
@Lazy public List<Contact> enabledContacts = contacts.findAll { contact ->
    contact.enabled
}

public Customer(Integer id,
                String name,
                String state,
                String domain,
                Boolean enabled,
                Contract contract,
                List<Contact> contacts) {
    this.id = id;
    this.name = name;
    this.state = state;
    this.domain = domain;
    this.enabled = enabled;
    this.contract = contract;
    this.contacts = contacts;
}

static def EnabledCustomer = { customer -> customer.enabled == true }
static def DisabledCustomer = { customer -> customer.enabled == false }

public static List<String> getDisabledCustomerNames() {
    Customer.allCustomers.findAll(DisabledCustomer).collect({cutomer ->
        cutomer.name
    })
}

public static List<String> getEnabledCustomerStates() {
    Customer.allCustomers.findAll(EnabledCustomer).collect({cutomer ->
        cutomer.state
    })
}

public static List<String> getEnabledCustomerDomains() {
    Customer.allCustomers.findAll(EnabledCustomer).collect({cutomer ->
        cutomer.domain
    })
}

public static List<String> getEnabledCustomerSomeoneEmail(String someone) {
    Customer.allCustomers.findAll(EnabledCustomer).collect({cutomer ->
        someone + "@" + cutomer.domain
    })
}
```

```
public static ArrayList<Customer> getCustomerById(
        ArrayList<Customer> inList,
        final Integer id) {
    inList.findAll({customer -> customer.id == id })
}

public static void eachEnabledContact(Closure cls) {
    Customer.allCustomers.findAll { customer ->
        customer.enabled && customer.contract.enabled
    }.each { customer ->
        customer.contacts.each(cls)
    }
}

public static List<Customer> updateCustomerByIdList(
        List<Customer> initialIds,
        List<Integer> ids,
        Closure cls) {
    if(ids.size() <= 0) {
        initialIds
    } else if(initialIds.size() <= 0) {
        []
    } else {
        def idx = ids.indexOf(initialIds[0].id)
        def cust = idx >= 0 ? cls(initialIds[0]) : initialIds[0]
        [cust] + updateCustomerByIdList(
            initialIds.drop(1),
            idx >= 0 ? ids.minus(initialIds[0].id) : ids,
            cls
        )
    }
}

public static List<Customer> updateContactForCustomerContact(
        Integer id,
        Integer contact_id,
        Closure cls) {
    updateCustomerByIdList(Customer.allCustomers, [id], { customer ->
        new Customer(
            customer.id,
            customer.name,
            customer.state,
            customer.domain,
            customer.enabled,
            customer.contract,
            customer.contacts.collect { contact ->
                if(contact.contact_id == contact_id) {
                    cls(contact)
                } else {
                    contact
                }
            }
```

```
                )
        })
    }

    public static List<Customer> updateContractForCustomerList(
            List<Integer> ids,
            Closure cls) {
        updateCustomerByIdList(Customer.allCustomers, ids, { customer ->
            new Customer(
                customer.id,
                customer.name,
                customer.state,
                customer.domain,
                customer.enabled,
                cls(customer.contract),
                customer.contacts
            )
        })
    }

    public static def countEnabledCustomersWithNoEnabledContacts = {
                    List<Customer> customers, Integer sum ->
        if(customers.isEmpty()) {
            return sum
        } else {
            int addition = (customers.head().enabled &&
                (customers.head().contacts.find({ contact ->
                    contact.enabled
                }) == null)) ? 1 : 0
            return countEnabledCustomersWithNoEnabledContacts.trampoline(
                customers.tail(),
                addition + sum
            )
        }
    }.trampoline()
}
```

When we convert the class and object over to Scala (see Example 7-9), there is one thing that doesn't work: there is no ternary operator! Remember (conditional) ? true : false? Well, as you can see in the Scala file, we actually replaced it with a true if statement.

Scala does not include the concept of ternary because everything already *is* a statement. This means that our if statement will evaluate to something. We can actually write if(conditional) { true } else { false } and the if statement will evaluate to either true or false.

Example 7-9. Customer.scala file

```scala
object Customer {

  val allCustomers = List[Customer]()

  def EnabledCustomer(customer : Customer) : Boolean = customer.enabled == true
  def DisabledCustomer(customer : Customer) : Boolean = customer.enabled == false

  def getDisabledCustomerNames() : List[String] = {
    Customer.allCustomers.filter(DisabledCustomer).map({ customer =>
      customer.name
    })
  }

  def getEnabledCustomerStates() : List[String] = {
    Customer.allCustomers.filter(EnabledCustomer).map({ customer =>
      customer.state
    })
  }

  def getEnabledCustomerDomains() : List[String] = {
    Customer.allCustomers.filter(EnabledCustomer).map({ customer =>
      customer.domain
    })
  }

  def getEnabledCustomerSomeoneEmail(someone : String) : List[String] = {
    Customer.allCustomers.filter(EnabledCustomer).map({ customer =>
      someone + "@" + customer.domain
    })
  }

  def getCustomerById(inList : List[Customer],
                      customer_id : Integer) : List[Customer] = {
    inList.filter(customer => customer.customer_id == customer_id)
  }

  def eachEnabledContact(cls : Contact => Unit) {
    Customer.allCustomers.filter({ customer =>
      customer.enabled && customer.contract.enabled
    }).foreach({ customer =>
      customer.contacts.foreach(cls)
    })
  }

  def updateCustomerByIdList(initialIds : List[Customer],
                             ids : List[Integer],
                             cls : Customer => Customer) : List[Customer] = {
    if(ids.size <= 0) {
      initialIds
    } else if(initialIds.size <= 0) {
      List()
```

```
    } else {
      val precust = initialIds.find(cust => cust.customer_id == ids(0))
      val cust = if(precust.isEmpty) { List() } else { List(cls(precust.get)) }
      cust ::: updateCustomerByIdList(
        initialIds.filter(cust => cust.customer_id == ids(0)),
        ids.drop(1),
        cls
      )
    }
  }
}

def updateContactForCustomerContact(customer_id : Integer,
                                    contact_id : Integer,
                                    cls : Contact => Contact) : List[Customer] = {
  updateCustomerByIdList(Customer.allCustomers, List(customer_id), { customer =>
    new Customer(
      customer.customer_id,
      customer.name,
      customer.state,
      customer.domain,
      customer.enabled,
      customer.contract,
      customer.contacts.map { contact =>
        if(contact.contact_id == contact_id) {
          cls(contact)
        } else {
          contact
        }
      }
    )
  })
}

def updateContractForCustomerList(ids : List[Integer],
                                  cls : Contract => Contract) : List[Customer] = {
  updateCustomerByIdList(Customer.allCustomers, ids, { customer =>
    new Customer(
      customer.customer_id,
      customer.name,
      customer.state,
      customer.domain,
      customer.enabled,
      cls(customer.contract),
      customer.contacts
    )
  })
}

def countEnabledCustomersWithNoEnabledContacts(customers : List[Customer],
                                               sum : Integer) : Integer = {
  if(customers.isEmpty) {
    sum
```

```
    } else {
      val addition = if(customers.head.enabled &&
                        customers.head.contacts.exists({ contact =>
                                                        contact.enabled
                                                      })) {
        1
      } else {
        0
      }
      countEnabledCustomersWithNoEnabledContacts(customers.tail, addition + sum)
    }
  }
}

class Customer(val customer_id : Integer,
               val name : String,
               val state : String,
               val domain : String,
               val enabled : Boolean,
               val contract : Contract,
               val contacts : List[Contact]) {
}
```

Let's look further into the code in Example 7-10, which shows how we can set a variable based on an if statement.

Example 7-10. if statement result returned

```
val addition = if(customers.head.enabled &&
    customers.head.contacts.exists({ contact => contact.enabled })) {
  1
} else {
  0
}
```

As we can see, `addition` will actually get 1 or 0 depending on the if evaluation. So, why is this much more interesting than a ternary? Because the `if` functions like a normal `if` statement, which means you can add any amount of code inside the `true` or `false` sections of the `if` statement. The ternary operator really only allows very simple expressions, such as a value or a basic method call.

But what do I really mean by "everything is a statement"? Well, I actually mean that everything should evaluate to something. But what exactly does *that* mean? Many of us know the normal *bean* methodology in Java—that is, having a member variable with getters and setters. Obviously, the getter will return some value, but what about the setter? Check out Example 7-11.

Example 7-11. A setter for the Foo field on the Bar class, which returns the object itself

```
public class Bar {
  public Bar setFoo(Foo foo) { this.foo = foo; return this; }
  public Foo getFoo() { return this.foo; }
}
```

This makes it possible for us to chain the function calls together and set a bunch of members in one line, as shown in Example 7-12. But why would we want to do this? Simply put, by doing this, we can redefine the setter methods and create immutable variables. Why? Because inside our setter, we can create a new instance of Bar with the new value and return that! This means that implementing immutable variables becomes simpler.

Example 7-12. Method chaining on the Bar object

```
return bar.setFoo(newFoo).setBaz(newBaz).setQux(newQux);
```

What about things like for loops—are those statements as well? As a matter of fact, yes, they are, but not in the way you might imagine. for loops generally come in two forms: one is just a normal loop, whereas the other is called a *comprehension*. The first type of loop is shown in Example 7-13.

Example 7-13. A basic for loop example in Scala

```
val x = for(i <- 0 until 10) {
  println(i)
}
```

When we run this code, we actually end up printing 0 to 9 on the screen. More important, the variable x is actually being set to something; in this case, it's being set to Unit.

That might sound strange, but in Scala, Unit is effectively a void type (meaning it has no actual type). This means that our for loop actually evaluated to nothing. So what are comprehensions? Let's look at a for comprehension in Example 7-14.

Example 7-14. A basic for comprehension in Scala

```
val x = for(i <- 0 until 10) yield {
  i*2
}
```

Now, we have an x that is a list from 0 to 18 by twos. The comprehension allows us to generate a new list of something, or sometimes iterate over another list. Let's look at Example 7-15, in which we're actually iterating over another list.

Example 7-15. A for comprehension over another list in Scala

```
val x = for(i <- List(1,2,3,4)) yield {
  i*2
}
```

So, what is the difference between this and using a `map` function on the list? Check out Example 7-16. This functionality is identical to the `for` comprehension in Example 7-15.

Example 7-16. A map call on a list in Scala

```
val x = List(1,2,3,4).map({ i => i*2 })
```

This begs the question, when do you use a `map` function versus a `for` comprehension? Generally, a `map` is good if you already have a list and need to perform an operation over it. `for` comprehensions are good if you are building a list or if need to do an operation *n* number of times.

Conclusion

We've taken the time to migrate from Java to Scala, marking our transition into a functional language that we'll be able to use in the upcoming chapters. Statements allowed us to reduce some of our code base and, in some instances, are necessary for us to still use some of our Java "bean" paradigms. We've seen in examples such as the `Calendar` object that when we need to use setters, we can create a block statement to set up our `Calendar`.

Statements also show us that every method should have some form of return value, even setters. And if we have setters that are statements, we can more easily implement immutable variables. Statements also make our code concise by forcing us to think about why we are writing a specific line of code and what that line of code is supposed to represent when evaluated. By doing this, we can better understand why a line of code acts the way that it does.

CHAPTER 8

Pattern Matching

Mostly when we, as programmers, think of *pattern matching* we think of regular expressions. But in the context of functional programming, this terminology takes on a new meaning. Instead of regular expression matching, we're going to be looking at matching objects against other objects.

Using pattern matching, you can extract from objects, match on members of objects, and verify that objects are of specific types—all within a statement. Pattern matching allows for fewer lines of variable assignment and more lines of understandable code. With pattern matching, you can match on members of an object, which allows you to write more concise logic for *when* a specific segment of code should be executed.

Simple Matches

Now that the code has started shaping up, our boss has asked us to create a new function that will create a new Customer. The requirements are as follows:

- name cannot be blank.
- state cannot be blank.
- domain cannot be blank.
- enabled must be true to start with.
- contract will be created based on today's date.
- contacts should be created as a blank list for now.

Our basic method, as shown in Example 8-1, uses a large if structure to return null in the event that an invalid value is passed in. We're currently printing to the console, but we should also log the message being sent.

Example 8-1. Imperative createCustomer method using an if structure

```
if(name.isEmpty) {
  println("Name cannot be blank")
  null
} else if(state.isEmpty) {
  println("State cannot be blank")
  null
} else if(domain.isEmpty) {
  println("Domain cannot be blank")
  null
} else {
  new Customer(
    0,
    name,
    state,
    domain,
    true,
    new Contract(Calendar.getInstance, true),
    List()
  )
}
```

This is a huge `if` structure that we do not want to maintain. Think back to Chapter 1, in which we were creating extractors from our `Customer` objects by using an `if` statement. We're almost doing the same thing here, using a giant `if` structure to determine whether certain fields are blank. By the end of our examples, we're going to see how this will become a much more manageable check.

For now, let's perform a simple refactor by using a very basic pattern match in Example 8-2. Using a pattern match is fairly straightforward in this instance: we're going to *match* each of our elements against a blank string, `""`.

The variable before the `match` keyword is what we'll pattern-match against. Inside the `match` statement are all of the patterns that we're going to test against, each defined with the `case` keyword. Right now, we just have `""`, which indicates a blank string, and the underscore _, which indicates *anything*.

Example 8-2. Very basic pattern match inside createCustomer

```
def createCustomer(name : String, state : String, domain : String) : Customer = {
  name match {
    case "" => {
      println("Name cannot be blank")
      null
    }
    case _ => state match {
      case "" => {
        println("State cannot be blank")
        null
      }
```

```
        case _ => domain match {
          case "" => {
            println("Domain cannot be blank")
            null
          }
          case _ => new Customer(
            0,
            name,
            state,
            domain,
            true,
            new Contract(Calendar.getInstance, true),
            List()
          )
        }
      }
    }
  }
}
```

Remember, we're transitioning to a better pattern match, so our first step has been to re-create the if/else structure, but in a pattern-match style. At first it seems like this has created an even larger mess, but don't worry: we're going to reduce the complexity quite a bit in the next sections.

Simple Patterns

Let's modify the pattern match that we created in createCustomer to be only one level deep. We can do this by creating a *tuple* (a group of elements) that we can then match against. Let's see this refactor in Example 8-3.

We are now defining a tuple (name, state, domain) against which we're going to match. What is so different here is that now we can match against each *part* of the tuple. We do this with case ("", _, _) which lets us say that this pattern should be a tuple with a blank string as the first value, and we don't care what the other two are.

Example 8-3. Collapsed pattern match to handle input validations

```
def createCustomer(name : String, state : String, domain : String) : Customer = {
  (name, state, domain) match {
    case ("", _, _) => {
      println("Name cannot be blank")
      null
    }
    case (_, "", _) => {
      println("State cannot be blank")
      null
    }
    case (_, _, "") => {
      println("Domain cannot be blank")
      null
```

```
    }
    case _ => new Customer(
        0,
        name,
        state,
        domain,
        true,
        new Contract(Calendar.getInstance, true),
        List()
      )
  }
}
```

Now that we have a way to convert `if` statements into pattern matches, let's see if we can convert another large `if`/`else` structure in our code base. Let's look at the original `setContractForCustomerList` method, shown in Example 8-4, which handles blank `initialIds` and `ids` parameters with a large `if` statement. Inside the `else`, we find the original `Customer` by id; if the customer is defined, we will execute our `cls` to update the `Customer`, putting it into a list. We then merge the list containing our updated `Customer` with the return of the recursive call.

Example 8-4. The original updateCustomerByIdList method

```
def updateCustomerByIdList(initialIds : List[Customer],
                           ids : List[Integer],
                           cls : Customer => Customer) : List[Customer] = {
  if(ids.size <= 0) {
    initialIds
  } else if(initialIds.size <= 0) {
    initialIds
  } else {
    val precust = initialIds.find(cust => cust.customer_id == ids(0))
    val cust = if(precust.isEmpty) { List() } else { List(cls(precust.get)) }
    cust ::: updateCustomerByIdList(
      initialIds.filter(cust => cust.customer_id == ids(0)),
      ids.tail,
      cls
    )
  }
}
```

We know how to handle this via pattern matching, so let's wrap those two variables into a *tuple* and match against a blank list. Much like our blank string `""`, we can imitate the blank list with `List()`, as shown in Example 8-5.

Example 8-5. Converting the original if/else structure into a pattern match

```
def updateCustomerByIdList(initialIds : List[Customer],
                           ids : List[Integer],
                           cls : Customer => Customer) : List[Customer] = {
  (initialIds, ids) match {
    case (List(), _) => initialIds
    case (_, List()) => initialIds
    case _ => {
      val precust = initialIds.find(cust => cust.customer_id == ids(0))
      val cust = if(precust.isEmpty) { List() } else { List(cls(precust.get)) }
      cust ::: updateCustomerByIdList(
        initialIds.filter(cust => cust.customer_id == ids(0)),
        ids.drop(1),
        cls
      )
    }
  }
}
```

But can we reduce the complexity of this method even further? Yes—by introducing extractors, specifically list extractors.

Extracting Lists

As their name implies, you can use extractors to pattern-match based on the object and *extract* members from the object itself. We'll see how to extract elements out of objects in the next section, but right now let's look at extracting from a list.

As you might recall, lists have a *head* and a *tail*, and we should be able to move through our list one item at a time by looking at the *head* and passing the *tail* to look at later. So let's check out the list extraction in Example 8-6 to see how we can move through our ids variable.

The :: operator, when used in a case statement, tells Scala that a list is expected and that the list should be *decomposed* into its head element (to the left of the operator) and its tail element (to the right of the operator). The variables into which the items are extracted exist only during the specific pattern execution.

The case (_, id :: tailIds) pattern will extract the head of the ids variable into a new variable called id and the tail of the ids into a new variable called tailIds.

Example 8-6. Extracting the head and tail from a list

```
def updateCustomerByIdList(initialIds : List[Customer],
                           ids : List[Integer],
                           cls : Customer => Customer) : List[Customer] = {
  (initialIds, ids) match {
    case (List(), _) => initialIds
    case (_, List()) => initialIds
```

```
      case (_, id :: tailIds) => {
        val precust = initialIds.find(cust => cust.customer_id == id)
        val cust = if(precust.isEmpty) { List() } else { List(cls(precust.get)) }
        cust ::: updateCustomerByIdList(
          initialIds.filter(cust => cust.customer_id == id),
          tailIds,
          cls
        )
      }
    }
  }
}
```

We're going to convert the find return into a list and then pattern-match against it. There are two possibilities here: either we will have a blank list, or we want the head element from the list itself. Let's look at the code in Example 8-7, in which we are doing this match.

The find return is being converted into a list for us to match against. We then perform the match on that and determine whether the list is blank or has elements (in which case we take the first one).

Example 8-7. Extracting the found customer during the find call

```
def updateCustomerByIdList(initialIds : List[Customer],
                           ids : List[Integer],
                           cls : Customer => Customer) : List[Customer] = {
  (initialIds, ids) match {
    case (List(), _) => initialIds
    case (_, List()) => initialIds
    case (_, id :: tailIds) => {
      val precust = initialIds.find(cust => cust.customer_id == id).toList
      precust match {
        case List() => updateCustomerByIdList(initialIds, tailIds, cls)
        case cust :: custs => updateCustomerByIdList(
          initialIds.filter(cust => cust.customer_id == id),
          tailIds,
          cls
        )
      }
    }
  }
}
```

So, why are we converting the return of find to a list? Well, the find method returns an Option, which is a generic interface that has two implementing classes: Some or None. As you might have guessed, the Some class will actually contain the object, whereas the None object contains nothing. We can convert the Option object to a List, which we can then pattern-match against.

However, we can actually pattern-match against the Option interface and reduce the need to convert it to a list. We'll get rid of our precust variable as well as the toList conversion. Instead, we're just going to send the find result directly to our pattern match.

We will create two case statements: one to match on the None object, and the other to match on Some. Notice in Example 8-8 that when we match on Some, we can use the syntax Some(cust), which allows us to extract the member of Some into our own variable, cust.

Example 8-8. Using the pattern match

```
def updateCustomerByIdList(initialIds : List[Customer],
                           ids : List[Integer],
                           cls : Customer => Customer) : List[Customer] = {
  (initialIds, ids) match {
    case (List(), _) => initialIds
    case (_, List()) => initialIds
    case (_, id :: tailIds) => {
      initialIds.find(cust => cust.customer_id == id) match {
        case None => updateCustomerByIdList(initialIds, tailIds, cls)
        case Some(cust) => updateCustomerByIdList(
          initialIds.filter(cust => cust.customer_id == id),
          tailIds,
          cls
        )
      }
    }
  }
}
```

What is that Some class, and how is it that we are able to extract members of the objects into variables? The Some class is actually a case class, and as we'll see in the next section, we can actually match and extract members of case classes.

Extracting Objects

Pattern matching includes the idea of matching on objects and extracting the fields from an object. As we've already seen in some of our examples, the *Option pattern* allows us to indicate either None or Some. With Some, we can encapsulate and get some value without having to write an if structure like the one shown in Example 8-9.

Example 8-9. How to handle the Option pattern in an if structure

```
var foo : Option[String] = Some("Bar")
if(obj.isDefined) {
  obj.get
} else {
```

```
    "" /* Not defined */
}
```

Instead, we can write a pattern match against `Option` and make it much more readable, as shown in Example 8-10.

Example 8-10. How to handle the Option pattern in a pattern match

```
var foo : Option[String] = Some("Bar")
obj match {
  case None => ""
  case Some(o) => o
}
```

We no longer have to write any `if` statements to compare types or `isDefined` calls. Instead, the pattern match handles the object comparison for us. We can do even more matches by looking inside the object, much as we did with the `Option` example. Let's say we have a `Some` object with the contents `Bar`. We can use the `case` syntax of `case Some("Bar")` to match on the value inside the `case` object. Let's see this in Example 8-11.

Example 8-11. How to handle a specific value inside a case object

```
var foo : Option[String] = Some("Bar")
obj match {
  case None => ""
  case Some("Bar") => "Foo"
  case Some(o) => o
}
```

What is really interesting about this Option pattern is that we can use it in our `create Customer` method. Remember the function in Example 8-3? Well, we can actually improve it by returning a `None` object (which does extend `Option`) on error, and returning `Some` if successful. Let's see this in Example 8-12.

Example 8-12. Returning the Option pattern

```
def createCustomer(name : String,
                   state : String,
                   domain : String) : Option[Customer] = {
  (name, state, domain) match {
    case ("", _, _) => {
      println("Name cannot be blank")
      None
    }
    case (_, "", _) => {
      println("State cannot be blank")
      None
    }
    case (_, _, "") => {
      println("Domain cannot be blank")
      None
```

```
    }
    case _ => new Some(new Customer(
        0,
        name,
        state,
        domain,
        true,
        new Contract(Calendar.getInstance, true),
        List()
      )
    )
  }
}
```

Here is the really interesting thing: we can actually make this more functional and encapsulate the print statement (logging) and return None because there is no reason to repeat ourselves. We can extract this into an error function that only needs to exist inside the createCustomer function. See the refactored code in Example 8-13.

Example 8-13. Extracting the logging of an error and returning of the option

```
def createCustomer(name : String,
                   state : String,
                   domain : String) : Option[Customer] = {
  def error(message : String) : Option[Customer] = {
    println(message)
    None
  }
  (name, state, domain) match {
    case ("", _, _) => error("Name cannot be blank")
    case (_, "", _) => error("State cannot be blank")
    case (_, _, "") => error("Domain cannot be blank")
    case _ => new Some(new Customer(
        0,
        name,
        state,
        domain,
        true,
        new Contract(Calendar.getInstance, true),
        List()
      )
    )
  }
}
```

Converting to Pattern Matches

There's another scenario in which converting from an if structure to a pattern match would actually increase readability. Let's look at the original countEnabledCustomers WithNoEnabledContacts method shown in Example 8-14.

Example 8-14. The original countEnabledCustomersWithNoEnabledContacts

```
def countEnabledCustomersWithNoEnabledContacts(customers : List[Customer],
                                               sum : Integer) : Integer = {
  if(customers.isEmpty) {
    sum
  } else {
    val addition = if(customers.head.enabled &&
                    customers.head.contacts.exists({ contact =>
                                                    contact.enabled
                                                  })) {
        1
      } else {
        0
      }
    countEnabledCustomersWithNoEnabledContacts(customers.tail, addition + sum)
  }
}
```

Now that we know how to extract from lists, we will try to rewrite this function. The first thing to do is define our Customer object as a case class, as shown in Example 8-15, by simply adding the case keyword to the class keyword.

Example 8-15. The Customer class defined as a case class

```
case class Customer(val customer_id : Integer,
                    val name : String,
                    val state : String,
                    val domain : String,
                    val enabled : Boolean,
                    val contract : Contract,
                    val contacts : List[Contact]) {
}
```

Now let's look at Example 8-16. Notice that we are going to handle the empty list first, then use the same type of syntax with the Some() object, except here we extract only the enabled and contacts of the Customer and ignore the rest.

For the enabled field, we want to match only if true is set for that field. We also want to pull out the Contact list into the cont variable.

Next, we have an if statement before our =>, which is called a *guard*. It allows us to match a pattern but only if a specific condition occurs. Finally, we call back into our function with the tail of our list and our *sum* + 1.

Example 8-16. A pattern match based on the customer being enabled

```
def countEnabledCustomersWithNoEnabledContacts(customers : List[Customer],
                                               sum : Integer) : Integer = {
  customers match {
    case List() => sum
    case Customer(_,_,_,_,true,_,cont) :: custs
        if cont.exists({ contact => contact.enabled}) =>
      countEnabledCustomersWithNoEnabledContacts(custs, sum + 1)
    case cust :: custs => countEnabledCustomersWithNoEnabledContacts(custs, sum)
  }
}
```

Now we can make this more efficient fairly easily: we can add a pattern to skip over our Contact list for the customer if it is blank, as shown in Example 8-17.

Example 8-17. A pattern match based on the customer being enabled and adding a check for a blank Contact list

```
def countEnabledCustomersWithNoEnabledContacts(customers : List[Customer],
                                               sum : Integer) : Integer = {
  customers match {
    case List() => sum
    case Customer(_,_,_,_,true,_,List()) :: custs =>
      countEnabledCustomersWithNoEnabledContacts(custs, sum)
    case Customer(_,_,_,_,true,_,cont) :: custs
        if cont.exists({ contact => contact.enabled}) =>
      countEnabledCustomersWithNoEnabledContacts(custs, sum + 1)
    case cust :: custs => countEnabledCustomersWithNoEnabledContacts(custs, sum)
  }
}
```

Conclusion

Throughout this chapter we've done quite a bit with pattern matching; we've actually converted our if structures into pattern matches. This has enabled us to perform simpler recursive loops over lists by using extractions from the lists. We have also been able to simplify our cases by matching on members inside the objects to reduce the amount of logic that we need to write.

We've also learned about the Option pattern, which allows us to get away from null objects by handling cases through pattern matching and either extracting the Some or handling a None case, as appropriate.

CHAPTER 9

Functional OOP

Dealing with immutable variables brings up an interesting question as we dive into object-oriented programming (OOP): "Why would we have an object if we're never going to change it?" This is where I've seen many people have an epiphany about functional programming. They understand the concept that an object is no longer something that "acts"; instead, it "contains" data.

As we go through this chapter, my hope is that you'll also understand that objects are merely containers that encapsulate a set of data. We'll answer the question "How does work get done?" by using static functions that will take our objects.

Back at XXY, your boss has asked you to extract the "send email" logic so that you can send emails for any type of report that might be requested in the future. He wants this to be done such that no other code that already calls sendEmail() has to be modified.

Static Encapsulation

Let's begin by refactoring. Your boss wants you to extract the def sendEmail() function so that the functionality can be reused. Let's first look at the Contact class and the corresponding def sendEmail() function that we will be migrating, as shown in Example 9-1.

Example 9-1. Send Email original

```
class Contact(val contact_id : Integer,
              val firstName : String,
              val lastName : String,
              val email : String,
              val enabled : Boolean) {

  def sendEmail() = {
      println("To: " + email + "\nSubject: My Subject\nBody: My Body")
  }

}
```

Let's begin extracting this functionality by creating a function that will take an Email object. Let's define our Email class, which will contain three members: address, sub ject, and body. It will also contain a send() method, which will call the Email.send method. The code in Example 9-2 shows our new class.

Example 9-2. Our new Email class

```
case class Email(val address : String,
                 val subject : String,
                 val body : String) {

  def send() : Boolean = Email.send(this)

}
```

Now, we can write our function itself. We will create the function send, which takes an Email object. For those not familiar with Scala, the code in Example 9-3 will seem odd with an object definition. An object is a singleton; it's where we will normally keep our static methods.

The body of our function will actually be the body of the original sendEmail function from our Email class. We've extracted this send function into our Email singleton, as shown in Example 9-3.

Example 9-3. Our new Email object

```
object Email {

  def send(msg : Email) : Boolean = {
    println("To: " + msg.address + "\nSubject: " + msg.subject +
            "\nBody: " + msg.body)
    true
  }

}
```

We've kept encapsulation by moving the send function into the Email singleton, allowing us to keep the email functionality within the Email object. We can now modify the sendEmail method in Contact to create a new Email object and then call its send() method, as shown in Example 9-4.

Example 9-4. Refactored Contact class

```
class Contact(val contact_id : Integer,
              val firstName : String,
              val lastName : String,
              val email : String,
              val enabled : Boolean) {

  def sendEmail() = {
    new Email(email, "My Subject", "My Body").send()
  }

}
```

Now you can see that our Email class has become nothing more than a container of the data itself; it has a minimal amount of code inside the class. We're calling into the Email singleton to perform the actual email functionality. How do objects as containers actually change how we see functions and data?

Objects As Containers

Your boss has requested that certain emails contain the name of a Contact in the format "Dear <name>". We'll add two parameters to our Email object, isDearReader and name. isDearReader indicates whether we should use the format, and name is the name we will use when sending the email. In Example 9-5, you can see our new Email class with the added fields.

Example 9-5. The Email class with isDearReader and name fields

```
case class Email(val address : String,
                 val subject : String,
                 val body : String,
                 val isDearReader : Boolean,
                 val name : String) {

  def send() : Boolean = Email.send(this)

}
```

Next we'll update the Email object to use these new parameters. In Example 9-6, we'll update the send method. We'll do this with an if statement to test if the isDearRead er field is true. If it is, we'll append the name field to our output.

Example 9-6. The Email object using isDearReader and name fields

```scala
object Email {

  def send(msg : Email) : Boolean = {
    if(msg.isDearReader) {
      println("To: " + msg.address + "\nSubject: " + msg.subject +
              "\nBody: Dear " + msg.name + ",\n" + msg.body)
    } else {
      println("To: " + msg.address + "\nSubject: " + msg.subject +
              "\nBody: " + msg.body)
    }
    true
  }

}
```

We can refactor this even further by using pattern matching. By using a pattern match on the `msg` variable, we will have two `case` statements: one for when `isDearReader` is `true`, and the other for when `isDearReader` is any other value. This refactor is shown in Example 9-7.

Example 9-7. The Email object with isDearReader using a pattern match

```scala
object Email {
  def send(msg : Email) : Boolean = {
    msg match {
      case Email(address, subject, body, true, name) =>
        println("To: " + address + "\nSubject: " + subject +
                "\nBody: Dear " + name + ",\n" + body)
      case Email(address, subject, body, _) =>
        println("To: " + address + "\nSubject: " + subject +
                "\nBody: " + body)
    }
    true
  }
}
```

We can refactor this further still by creating a `send` method that takes the `to`, `subject`, and body fields and performs the send. We have refactored this based on what we believe constitutes the most basic components of sending an email. Example 9-8 shows this refactoring.

Example 9-8. The Email object extracting the send function with common functionality

```scala
object Email {

  def send(to : String, subject : String, body : String) : Boolean = {
    println("To: " + to + "\nSubject: " + subject + "\nBody: " + body)
    true
  }
```

```
def send(msg : Email) : Boolean = {
  msg match {
    case Email(address, subject, body, true, name) =>
      send(address, subject, "Dear " + name + ",\n" + body)
    case Email(address, subject, body, _, _) =>
      send(address, subject, body)
  }
  true
  }
}
```

Now that we've updated the `Email` functionality, we need to update our `Contact.sen dEmail()` method so that we can take advantage of this new feature. Your boss has asked that any time you call `sendEmail()` on the contact, you should use the `isDearReader` functionality. We can now update our code as shown in Example 9-9.

Example 9-9. The Contact classes' sendEmail() method handling isDearReader

```
def sendEmail() = {
  new Email(this.email, "My Subject", "My Body", true, this.firstName).send()
}
```

Our `Email` class is now more of a container; its primary job is to contain all of the fields that are necessary for creating the email, not necessarily sending it. This illustrates the harmony that we really want between functional programming and OOP.

Code as Data

Back at XXY, your boss has asked that you allow for a way to create a customer from the command line. Thus we're going to create a new `CommandLine` object, which will actually have a few different functions:

- Display a question and get input from a user.
- Display all possible options to a user.
- Interpret a user's input.

Let's begin by creating a really simple class representing our command-line options. We'll call it `CommandLineOption`, and it will be a `case class`, as shown in Example 9-10. Our class will have a `description` and a function `func` to be executed when it is selected.

Extension of the Strategy Design Pattern
This method is fairly similar to the *Strategy* Java design pattern, except that we can directly pass a function rather than an implementing class of an interface.

Example 9-10. The CommandLineOption case class

```scala
case class CommandLineOption(description : String, func : () => Unit)
```

Next, let's create the `CommandLine` object, which will have two primary methods. The first will `askForInput` given some prompt, as shown in Example 9-11.

Example 9-11. The CommandLine.askForInput method

```scala
def askForInput(question : String) : String = {
  print(question + ": ")
  readLine()
}
```

Next, we will create a method that gives the user a `prompt` of options and asks her for input. The method will draw from the `options` variable, which will be of type `Map[String, CommandLineOption]` and will allow us to search the `Map` for the option that the user selects. Check out the `prompt` function in Example 9-12.

Example 9-12. The CommandLine.prompt method

```scala
def prompt() = {
  options.foreach(option => println(option._1 + ") " + option._2.description))
  options.get(askForInput("Option").trim.toLowerCase) match {
    case Some(CommandLineOption(_, exec)) => exec()
    case _ => println("Invalid input")
  }
}
```

Notice how we iterate over each `option`, printing out `._1` and accessing `._2.descrip` `tion`. The `_1` refers to the first option of the `Map` (the `String`), whereas the `_2` refers to the second option (the `CommandLineOption`).

Next, we `askForInput` and then search the `options` variable for the option. We will have either `Some`, in which case we extract the `func` from our `CommandLineOption` class, or we will have `None`, for which we assume the user gave us bad input.

So, what does this `options` variable look like? It's actually really simple: we build a `Map` (indicated by a *<key> -> <value>* syntax) containing the `option` that the user will input (as the key), and the `CommandLineOption` object (as the value). The definition of all of our existing options is shown in Example 9-13.

Example 9-13. The CommandLine.options variable

```scala
val options : Map[String, CommandLineOption] = Map(
  "1" -> new CommandLineOption("Add Customer", Customer.createCustomer),
  "2" -> new CommandLineOption("List Customers", Customer.list),
  "q" -> new CommandLineOption("Quit", sys.exit)
)
```

The beauty of being able to reference functions is that we can actually set a function from another `Object` as part of another function. Notice how we have two options, `Add Customer` and `List Customers`, that reference previously existing functions? This allows us to use a pre-existing function without breaking the encapsulation.

Your boss has come back to ask you to create an input option that allows users to view all enabled contacts for all enabled customers. This seems really straightforward. We already have a function, `eachEnabledContact`, that we can pass a function to and print out each contact!

Let's see what our function would look like to print out each enabled contact in Example 9-14. Here we will use our `eachEnabledContact` method and pass a function that takes a single argument and prints the variable.

Example 9-14. How Customer.eachEnabledContact would be used to print out the contacts

```
Customer.eachEnabledContact(contact => println(contact))
```

And if we needed that to be its own function, we would just use Scala's empty parentheses syntax, as in Example 9-15. This example defines a function that takes no arguments but executes the code in Example 9-14.

Example 9-15. Encapsulating the printing of each enabled contact as its own function

```
() => Customer.eachEnabledContact(contact => println(contact))
```

So, let's look at our new `options` variable in Example 9-16 and see how it works with our new option. We'll just continue down the line and add it as option 3.

Example 9-16. The CommandLine.options variable with the new "print each enabled contact" option added

```
val options : Map[String, CommandLineOption] = Map(
  "1" -> new CommandLineOption("Add Customer", Customer.createCustomer),
  "2" -> new CommandLineOption("List Customers", Customer.list),
  "3" -> new CommandLineOption("List Enabled Contacts for Enabled Customers",
    () => Customer.eachEnabledContact(contact => println(contact))
  ),
  "q" -> new CommandLineOption("Quit", sys.exit)
)
```

Conclusion

It's important to understand that functional programming itself is not a replacement for OOP; in fact, we can still use many OOP concepts. Objects are no longer used to encapsulate a large group of statements in an imperative manner, but instead are designed to encapsulate a set of variables into a common grouping.

We are able to expand concepts such as the *Command pattern* or the *State pattern* by just creating a class that contains a method to be defined later. This style of definition allows us to change the method at runtime without breaking encapsulation or having lots of erroneous classes living everywhere.

Think back to our CommandLineOption example: we created quite a few options by just passing functions to a new CommandLineOption. This allows us to create tons of objects extending from an abstract object without actually defining every type. We can also more easily implement patterns, such as the *Visitor pattern*, where Object A accepts Object B, and Object B does some operation on Object A.

Let's assume that we have a class Foo that has an accept method. But we're not going to accept another class; instead, we just accept the function that performs the visitor work we want to do. The visitor just becomes a simple function that we're passing to Foo. See Example 9-17.

Example 9-17. Visitor pattern using functions

```
class Foo {
  val value = "bar"
  def accept(func : Foo => Unit) = {
    func(this)
  }
}

new Foo().visit(f => println(f.value))
```

Now you can see that functional programming allows us to continue using many OOP concepts and ideas while reducing the number of classes we write. Where we would write classes to encapsulate a single function, we can now just send a function rather than an implementing class.

How about an example in which we implement a command pattern where we have a string transformer (take a string, transform it, return a string)? Think about how you would implement it and then check out Example 9-18.

Example 9-18. Command pattern using functions

```
def toUpperCase(str : String) : () => String = { () => str.toUpperCase }
def transform : () => String = toUpperCase("foo")
println(transform())
```

Notice that we no longer need to create separate objects, but instead we can just return the *command* as a function to execute. This decreases the number of classes we're creating and keeping track of, thus increasing the readability of our code.

CHAPTER 10

Conclusion

I hope that you've found this book to be a helpful stepping-stone toward functional programming. Most important, I hope that it has demystified some of the concepts and shown how you might implement them without switching to a purely functional language.

I also hope that you can take some of the early concepts that might actually provide you the greatest benefit and apply those to your everyday job, helping you write less code while implementing more functionality.

From Imperative to Functional

At this point, you should have the knowledge and the understanding of how to transform your current imperative code into functional code. As you start your transition, you will want to break it down into steps. Let's look at the transitional steps and recap how to implement those concepts:

1. Introduce *higher-order functions*.
2. Convert existing methods into pure functions.
3. Convert loops over to recursive/tail-recursive methods (if possible).
4. Convert mutable variables into immutable variables.
5. Use pattern matching (if possible).

Introduce Higher-Order Functions

The first step to take is to introduce some *higher-order functions*, as you saw in Chapter 2. To accomplish this in Java, you either use pre-existing libraries such as Guava or create your own interface like the `Function1` interface so that you can encapsulate functionality to be passed to another function.

As demonstrated in Chapter 2, you can also begin to convert to a language such as Groovy, which enables you to use higher-order functions while still keeping the basic Java syntax. The advantage is that you don't need to rewrite your entire code base in order to convert.

If you cannot integrate with a non-type-safe language such as Groovy, I would suggest starting to integrate with another language, such as Scala, to keep your type safety but still begin integrating functional concepts.

This has the largest benefit, because you'll be able to immediately start taking advantage of code reuse. You'll start seeing loops where you can abstract the looping logic and just start passing a higher-order function into the looping logic.

Convert Existing Methods into Pure Functions

The next step is to start converting your normal methods into pure functions, as I showed in Chapter 3. These should actually be fairly straightforward to convert—and as you begin converting them, you'll find how much easier it is to write tests for those functions.

This is, again, one step that will have a lot of benefit right up front. You'll begin to reduce your functions, which will make them even more testable and more understandable. This is really one of the first times that the concept of expressiveness will come up. As your decompose your functions into smaller, more pure functions, they will inherently become more *expressive*. Expressiveness reflects how much meaning each line of code has; the more that can be understood per one line of code, the more expressiveness it has.

Convert Loops to Tail/Recursive-Tail Methods

You don't want to jump directly into immutable variables, so the first thing to do is convert your looping structures over to recursive—specifically, tail-recursive if you can —methods. The caveat here is that some languages, such as Java, don't support tail recursion. If you can use it without worrying about buffer overflow, try it.

Recursion is something that many people find unfamiliar at first, but after you get into a functional mindset and practice with it, you'll get much better at seeing the conceptual framework. You'll see iteration via recursion instead of just normal iterative loops. The nice thing about recursion is that you'll be able to truly test your loops to make sure that you're looping over what you want. You'll also be able to more fully test them.

Convert Mutable Variables into Immutable Variables

One of the last things you can do—without switching to a fully functional language—is move your normal *mutable* variables into *immutable* variables. This has many different implications, including the ability to do highly concurrent applications without locking variables.

Immutable variables are one of the more difficult things to get used to working with because we, as developers, are so accustomed to changing variables over time. The positive for not changing the variable is that you have no concern that a variable has "changed out from under you."

What Next?

After you've done these things, generally you will have exhausted most of your functional abilities in the language you're using. The next step, then, is to move to a more functional language, such as Scala or Groovy, or to a fully functional language, such as Erlang or Clojure. Whatever you choose, the concepts and ways to program in the functional paradigm will remain the same.

New Design Patterns

There are a few different design patterns based on some of the concepts we've seen throughout this book:

- Message passing for concurrency (actor model for concurrency)
- The Option pattern (extension of Null Object pattern)
- Object to Singleton method purity

Let's look at some of these design patterns and how we can actually use them in our day-to-day jobs.

Message Passing for Concurrency

When we think about concurrency, we think about a thread that starts, processes an amount of work, and then exits. Sometimes we think of a *thread pool* to which we submit jobs to be executed. However, with message passing we can actually send a *message*, which is then interpreted by the running thread to do processing.

The big difference between message passing and thread pools is that with the latter, an individual job must be created and executed, whereas in message passing you can have a thread that exists for a long period of time, and send messages to that thread to tell it what operations to perform. This allows the threads to communicate without blocking.

The Option Pattern (Extension of Null Object Pattern)

The *Null Object pattern* in Java is a way you can provide an object to be executed, but the object does nothing when executed and thus removes the need for null. An extension of that pattern is the Option pattern. The concept, as we saw in earlier chapters, is that you have an Option interface that is implemented by a Some and a None case; then with pattern matching, you are able to extract when the Option has Some or do an else if there is None.

Even if we don't have pattern matching, we can still use the Option pattern by creating a getOrElse(T obj) method on the Option interface. This way, you can actually pass something to use in the event that you have None. All of the classes are listed in Example 10-1.

Example 10-1. The implementation of the Option pattern

```
public interface Option<T> {

        public T getOrElse(T defObj);

}

public class Some<T> implements Option<T> {

        private final T obj;

        public Some(T obj) {
                this.obj = obj;
        }

        public T getOrElse(T defObj) {
                return (this.obj == null) ? defObj : this.obj;
        }

}

public class None<T> implements Option<T> {

        public T getOrElse(T defObj) {
                return obj;
        }

}
```

Now we can use this by passing a new Some<String>("Foo") or a new None<String>(), which then forces the method accepting the Option<String> to do a getOrElse. This means that it will *always* check for nullity so long as the underlying object is not null.

Object to Singleton Method Purity

Generally in object-oriented programming (OOP), our functions will contain lots of functional logic. In many instances, this functionality may bleed throughout an entire class. This means that you will eventually need the class to be instantiated to test even the most basic functionality.

Instead, when we want to have a set of functionality, we should create our `static` methods and then have our instance methods call those directly. This allows us to maintain function purity while being able to have OOP expressiveness. Example 10-2 shows a method on the instance that *only* calls a `static` method.

Example 10-2. The singleton method purity

```
public class Foo {

  public static String bar(Foo f) { return f.toString(); }

  public String bar() { return Foo.bar(f); }

}
```

Putting It All Together

Throughout this book, I've tried to convey the principles of functional programming by showing you how to start with an imperative paradigm and move to the functional one. Instead of refactoring, we're going to put all of these principles into action by building an example from the ground up.

Over the next few pages, we're going to work through an example of a very simplistic database. Here is a very basic overview of the functionality that we'll be implementing; it will be a menu-driven system, so it's not meant to be a full-fledged database. It will have the following capabilities:

- Can create a table
- Can insert a record
- Can delete a record (by ID)
- Can list all records
- Can query by one field

We're going to use Scala, and we'll get started by working with the initial application object shown in Example 10-3.

Example 10-3. The fDB.scala file

```scala
import scala.annotation.tailrec

object fDB {

  val options = Map[String, CommandLineOption](
    "create" -> new CommandLineOption("Create Table", Database.createTable),
    "describe" -> new CommandLineOption("Describe Table", Database.describeTable),
    "insert" -> new CommandLineOption("Insert Record", Database.insert),
    "delete" -> new CommandLineOption("Delete Record", Database.delete),
    "select" -> new CommandLineOption("Select Record", Database.select),
    "exit" -> new CommandLineOption("Exit", db => sys.exit)
  )

  @tailrec
  def mainLoop(database : Database) : Unit = mainLoop(
    CommandLine.optionPrompt(options) match {
      case Some(opt) => opt.exec(database)
      case _ => { println("Invalid option"); database }
    }
  )

  def main(args : Array[String]) = {
      mainLoop(new Database(Map()))
  }

}
```

The variable options is a mapping of all the possible options that a user can enter. These options are create, describe, insert, delete, select, and exit. For each one, we'll create a CommandLineOption object, shown in Example 10-4, that contains a description and an executable function.

We'll also create a mainLoop that will execute the CommandLine (Example 10-5), which will prompt a user based on the options available and try to grab that Command LineOption.

If the option doesn't exist, we make no changes and let the user know that she selected an invalid option. Otherwise, we will execute the CommandLineOption executable function, which will perform the necessary changes to the Database object, and which we will continue using in our tail-recursive function.

Finally, we have our main function, which will call into our mainLoop with a new blank Database object.

In Example 10-4, you can see the basic CommandLineOption object. It contains a name to be used for display purposes so that the user knows *what* the option does, and the exec, which will take a Database object, perform some operation based on that object, and then return either that Database or a new one.

Example 10-4. The CommandLineOption.scala file

```scala
class CommandLineOption(val name : String, val exec : Database => Database)
```

The CommandLine object in Example 10-5 performs all of our prompting and printing functionality. We have a wrapOutput function, which will take some wrapping and some output that we want to display. We will then print the wrapping, followed by the out put and the wrapping again, so that we have a nice separation of data.

The next function is our optionPrompt function, which takes a mapping of *input* to CommandLineOption; this allows us to print out the mapping and then ask the user for the input. We will print in the format option) CommandLineOption.name and then ask the user to give us an input.

Our last function is a generic prompt function, which will print a message to the user and wait for her to input a line of data.

Example 10-5. The CommandLine.scala file

```scala
object CommandLine {

  def wrapOutput(wrapper : String, output : String) : Unit = {
    println(wrapper)
    print(output)
    println(wrapper)
  }

  def optionPrompt(options : Map[String, CommandLineOption]) :
                             Option[CommandLineOption] = {
    println()
    println("----[Options]----")
    options.foreach(option => println(option._1 + ") " + option._2.name))
    options.get(prompt("Action").toLowerCase)
  }

  def prompt(msg : String) : String = {
    print(msg + ": ")
    readLine()
  }

}
```

Our Database class in Example 10-6 is really straightforward—it has a set of tables, which will be a map of table name to Table. We'll discuss the Table object in Example 10-7; for now, get to the Database object (singleton).

Example 10-6. The Database.scala file

```scala
object Database {

  def createTable(database : Database) : Database = {
    new Database(database.tables +
                          (CommandLine.prompt("Table Name") -> Table.create()))
  }

  def describeTable(database : Database) : Database = {
    database.tables.get(CommandLine.prompt("Table Name")) match {
      case Some(table) => table.describe()
      case _ => println("Table does not exist")
    }
    database
  }

  def insert(database : Database) : Database = {
    val tableName = CommandLine.prompt("Table Name")
    database.tables.get(tableName) match {
      case Some(table) => {
        new Database(database.tables + (tableName -> table.insert()))
      }
      case _ => { println("Table does not exist"); database }
    }
  }

  def select(database : Database) : Database = {
    database.tables.get(CommandLine.prompt("Table Name")) match {
      case Some(table) => table.select()
      case _ => println("Table does not exist")
    }
    database
  }

  def delete(database : Database) : Database = {
    val tableName = CommandLine.prompt("Table Name")
    database.tables.get(tableName) match {
      case Some(table) => new Database(
                          database.tables + (tableName -> table.delete()))
      case _ => { println("Table does not exist"); database }
    }
  }
}

case class Database(tables : Map[String, Table]) {}
```

Our first method, `create`, will do just that—create a new table. We implement this by prompting for a table name that we will then use in our Table Name-to-Table mapping. We then use the function `create` to create a new table. You'll notice that we're adding this new association to our existing table mapping and creating a new `Database` object with this new table mapping.

Next, we have a `describeTable` method, which allows us to print out all of the fields from a specific table. Notice that we use the pattern match with the Option pattern to get the table by name and print an error if the table doesn't exist.

In the `insert` method, we get the table and create a new database with the table *replaced* in the map. The important thing here is that the table we're replacing it with will be the `Table` object's `insert` return in Example 10-7.

The `select` method gets the table from which the user wants to select; it then uses a pattern match on the Option pattern again to perform the select on that table or print an error if the table doesn't exist.

Finally, the `delete` method gets the table from which the user wants to delete, uses the pattern match on the Option pattern, and then passes to the table for the delete.

Our `Table` class in Example 10-7 has quite a few pieces to it. Let's look at the class first, and notice the use of the `static` method calls from the instance methods.

Example 10-7. The Table.scala file

```scala
object Table {

  def createFields(count : Int,
                   fields : List[String]) : List[String] = if(count <= 0) {
    fields
  } else {
    createFields(count - 1, fields ::: List(CommandLine.prompt("Field")))
  }

  def create() : Table = new Table(
    createFields(
      CommandLine.prompt("Number of fields").toInt,
      List()
    ),
    Map(),
    1
  )

  def insert(table : Table) : Table = new Table(
    table.fields,
    table.records + (table.id -> Record.create(table.fields, Map())),
    table.id + 1
  )

  def describe(table : Table) : Table = {
    println("(implied) id")
    table.fields.foreach(field => println(field))
    table
```

```
    }

    def select(table : Table) : Table = {
      CommandLine.prompt("Filter By Field? (y/n)").toLowerCase match {
        case "y" => selectWithFilter(table)
        case "n" => selectAll(table)
        case _ => { println("Invalid selection"); select(table); }
      }
    }

    def selectAll(table : Table) : Table = {
      table.records.foreach(record => record._2.print(table.fields, record._1))
      table
    }

    def selectWithFilter(table : Table) : Table = {
      performFilter(
        table,
        CommandLine.prompt("Filter Field"),
        CommandLine.prompt("Field Value")
      ).foreach(record =>
        record._2.print(table.fields, record._1)
      )
      table
    }

    def performFilter(table : Table,
                      fieldName : String,
                      fieldValue : String) : Map[Long, Record] = {
      if(fieldName == "id") {
        table.records.get(fieldValue.toLong) match {
          case Some(record) => Map(fieldValue.toLong -> record)
          case _ => Map()
        }
      } else {
        table.records.filter(record =>
          record._2.fieldValues.get(fieldName) match {
            case Some(value) => value == fieldValue
            case _ => false
          }
        )
      }
    }

  def delete(table : Table) : Table = {
    new Table(table.fields, table.records - CommandLine.prompt("ID").toLong, table.id)
  }

}

case class Table(fields : List[String], records : Map[Long, Record], id : Long) {
```

```
  def delete() : Table = {
    Table.delete(this)
  }

  def select() : Table = {
    Table.select(this)
  }

  def insert() : Table = {
    Table.insert(this)
  }

  def describe() : Table = {
    Table.describe(this)
  }

}
```

We have a createFields method that will create all of our fields in a tail-recursive manner. Notice that we don't actually need to use a pattern match to do tail recursion. We also have the create method, which asks for the number of fields and then calls into createFields to create the list of fields.

We also have an insert method, which will call into Record (shown in Example 10-8) to ask for each individual field value. We then add the record to our map with the id from the Table and create a new table with the new map and increment the id for the new table.

Our describe method iterates over each field and prints it out so that we know the table structure.

Next, we have our select method, which asks the user if she wants to filter the records for which she's looking. Depending on which option she selects, we will go into either selectAll or selectWithFilter.

The selectAll iterates over each record and calls print. The selectWithFilter asks the user which field she wants to filter on and the value for which she's looking. We then call into the performFilter method, which will return a map of only matching records and print out those records.

Our performFilter method splits on the field. If the user asks for the id field, we can directly access it based on the map's key; otherwise, we will perform a filter on the records map to find the records that match. Notice that we can pattern-match in the case that the field is *missing*, and instead of blowing up, we're just not going to match.

Finally, we have the delete method, which asks the user what id she wants to remove, and we remove it from the records map.

Our last `Record` class in Example 10-8 is fairly simple, but again let's look at the class first.

Example 10-8. The Record.scala file

```scala
object Record {

  def create(fields : List[String],
              fieldValues : Map[String, String]) : Record = fields match {
    case List() => new Record(fieldValues)
    case f :: fs =>
      create(
        fs,
        fieldValues + (f -> CommandLine.prompt("Value [" + f + "]"))
      )
  }

  def print(fields : List[String], id : Long, record : Record) : Unit = {
    def _print(fieldList : List[String], output : String) : String = fieldList match {
      case List() => output
      case f :: fs => _print(fs, output + f + ": " + record.fieldValues(f) + "\n")
    }
    CommandLine.wrapOutput("------------", "id: " + id + "\n" + _print(fields, ""))
  }

}

case class Record(fieldValues : Map[String, String]) {

  def print(fields : List[String], id : Long) : Unit = {
    Record.print(fields, id, this)
  }

}
```

We have a `print` method on the class itself that calls into the static `print` method, passing the list and `id` of the object along with itself.

In the singleton, we have two primary methods. The first is the `create` method, which uses tail recursion to iterate over the field list, asking for each field input. After all fields have been asked for, we create a new `Record` with the map we've been building through our recursive function.

The second method, `print`, takes the list of fields, the `id` of the record, and the record itself. We then create a nested function, `_print`, which does a tail-recursive iteration to create an output string that will contain each field and value. The `print` method uses the inner `_print` method and passes the output to our `CommandLine` object's `wrapOutput` method, which then nicely prints out the object.

We now have a small functional database that we can use for simple queries. Our database utilizes all of the concepts of functional programming—from higher-order functions to immutability.

Conclusion

Throughout this chapter, we covered how you can start making the transition from a legacy imperative style to a functional style of programming. We also looked at both new design patterns and extensions of existing design patterns.

Finally, we wrote a simple, functional database in Scala. In doing so, we used first-class functions and functional OOP through the use of our CommandLineOption object. We also used pattern matching to determine whether the input option was valid. In addition, we used pure functions, recursion, and immutability throughout the application. Even when creating/updating/deleting records, we were able to apply immutability using recursion.

Taking It a Step Further

Here are some ideas to consider if you want to try to expand upon this database concept:

- When selecting by field, add the ability to select by *regex* or *like*
- Add save/load functionality
- Turn the database into a client/server model
- Integrate error handling (most of it is done except the data input)
- Create transactional support (you'll notice with the immutable database, you already have some of this ready for use)

By completing more examples and forcing yourself to implement features based on functional concepts, you'll become a better functional programmer.

I've watched quite a few people start out programming in imperative style while trying to learn functional programming. At some point—sometimes it's while covering functional OOP concepts, and sometimes it's later—it "clicks" for people, and they start seeing code in loops and lists. They start thinking of functions as variables and begin to pass them around instead of just data. When you begin to pass around parts of the application itself, you open up the possibilities of your code and what you can accomplish.

Index

We'd like to hear your suggestions for improving our indexes. Send email to index@oreilly.com.

throwing for null return value, 27

extractors

extracting lists, 97

extracting objects, 99

F

filter function, 27, 56–58

abstracting and putting into singleton class, 35

basic, using recursion, 58

converting to tail-recursive call, 61

getCustomerById method using, 28

getField function using, 28

in Groovy, using iterative loop, 56

purifying, 29

simplified function using recursion, 58

final variables and @Lazy annotation (Groovy), 72

final, marking closed-over variables as, 19

find function return, converting to a list and pattern-matching against it, 98

first-class functions, 2, 5–24

anonymous functions, 16

closures, 18

lambda functions, 16

functions as objects, 7

refactoring using if-else structures, 8

using function objects to extract fields, 10

higher-order functions, 20

refactoring get functions using Groovy, 22

using in recursive summation, 55

XXY company (example), 5

Customer.java file, 5

DRY principle, 7

flatten() function, 68

for loops, 26

abstracting into a filter function, 28

as statements, 91

basic for loop in Scala (example), 91

for comprehension in Scala (example), 91

for comprehension over another list in Scala, 91

for comprehension versus map function, 92

summation in, 56

foreach function, 30

abstracting and putting into singleton class, 35

defined in Customer class (example), 31

side effects and, 35

function chaining

counting enabled customers with disabled contacts (example), 59

functional programming

and concurrency, 3

concepts in, 1

first-class functions, 2

immutable variables, 2

importance of, x

nonstrict evaluations, 2

pattern matching, 2

pure functions, 2

recursion, 2

statements, 2

taking the database concept further, 125

transforming imperative code into functional code, 113–115

using with OOP, ix, 105–112

versus imperative programming, ix

writing a simple functional database in Scala (example), 117–125

functional programming languages, 115

functions, viii

as objects, 7

using function objects to extract fields, 10

components of, 7

in Scala, 66

passing a mutable object to, 44

passing a mutable variable to, 44

referencing, 111

G

generic typing (Scala), 83

get functions, refactoring using Groovy, 22

getCustomerById() method (example), 26

in Groovy, 38

purifying, 30

using a filter function, 28

getDisabledCustomerNames() function (example)

refactoring in Groovy, 39

taking purity too far, 37

getEnabledCustomerField() function (example), 8

passing ConversionFunction object to, 11

using if-else structure, 9

with generic typed Function1, 13

getEnabledCustomerNames() function (example), 8

getters and setters, 90
Groovy, vii
    @Lazy annotation and final variables, 72
    converting to, 38
    dynamic typing, 38
    Filter function in, 56
    getCustomerById() function in, 38
    laziness problem in, 73
    lazy usage, good, example of, 74
    printing all contracts, 39
    refactoring other Customer.java code into, 39
    setContractEnabledForCustomer() method (example), 32
    setContractForCustomer method, 39
    syntax, 23
    TestClass with lazy member (example)
        and print statements, 70
        lazy member not evaluated until it's referenced, 71
    TestClass with nonlazy member (example), 70
        and print statements, 70
    updating contract field, 38
    using higher-order functions in, 114
    using to refactor get functions, 22
    volatile keyword, using with @Lazy annotation, 72
guard, 102

H

head (lists), 57
    extracting in Scala, 97
higher-order functions, 20
    defined, 23
    introducing, 113

I

if statements, viii, 2
    in recursiive function end case, 57
    in Scala, 66, 87
    using with getEnabledCustomerField function, 8
if/else structures
    converting to pattern matches
        countEnabledCustomersWithNoEnabledContacts method, 102

    in getEnabledCustomerField function (example), 8
    in Scala updateCustomerByIdList, converting to pattern matches, 96
    recreated in pattern-match style, 95
    using in Scala imperative createCustomer method, 93
immutability, 45, 48
    immutable Contract object, 50
    immutable Customer object, 49
    in recursive algorithm, 58
    maintained with nonstrict evaluation, 67
    mutable allCustomers list containing immutable Customer objects, 49
immutable variables, 2, 43–54
    benefits of using, 54
    converting mutable variables to, 115
imperative programming, ix
    transforming imperative code into functional code, 113–115
        changing to functional programming language, 115
        converting existing methods to pure functions, 114
        converting loops to tail/recursive-tail methods, 114
        converting mutable variables into immutable variables, 115
        introducing higher-order functions, 113
instance methods, 117
interfaces (Java)
    abstraction for higher-order function, 30
    creating abstraction of function to pass to another function, 10
    encapsulating functions, 12
isEmpty method (Scala), 66
iteration
    counting enabled customers with disabled contacts (example), 59
    iterative algorithms versus recursive, 56

J

Java, vii
    imperative programming, ix
    introducing higher-order functions, 113
    lazy variable, example of, 67
    method chaining (example), 91
    Null Object pattern, 116
    setter as statement (example), 90

simple assignment statement, 79
singleton method purity, 117
Strategy design pattern, 109

L

lambda functions, 16
 using to reduce number of inner classes, 16
lazy evaluations
 example of good usage in Groovy, 74
 example of good usage in Scala, 75
 laziness creating problems in Groovy, 73
lazy variables, 67
 definition in Scala, 72
LISP, 1
lists
 and for comprehensions in Scala, 91
 appending rather than prepending to output list, 62
 extracting from, 97
 Filter function end case with head creation, 57
 Filter function outputting tail of list, 58
 flattening, 68
 head and tail of, 57
 map function call on, in Scala, 92
looping, 10
 abstracting in updateCustomer and updateContract methods, 53
loops, converting to recursive methods, 114

M

macros, 7
map function, 35
 abstracting and putting into singleton class, 35
 map call on a list in Scala, 92
 versus a for comprehension, when to use, 92
match statement, 94
mathematical notation, viii
message passing for concurrency, 115
method chaining in Java, 91
mutability, 43–48
mutable variables, 43
 converting to immutable, 115
 passed to a function, modifying, 44

N

name (of a function), 7
None class, 98, 116
nonstrict evaluation, 2, 67
 Customer.enabledContacts method, 69
 Groovy TestClass with lazy member, 70
 laziness creating problems, 73
 lazy usage, good, in Scala, 75
 when and where to use, 76
Null Object pattern, 116
nullity, 27
 avoiding null as dangerous construct, 58
NullPointerException, 27
nulls, returning empty list instead of, 32

O

object to singleton method purity, 117
object-oriented programming (OOP)
 functional, 105–112
  code as data, 109
  objects as containers, 107
  static encapsulation, 105
 functional style with, ix
 functions in, 117
objects
 extracting, 99
 functions as, 5, 7
 Scala, 81
Option interface, 98, 116
Option pattern, 99, 116
 extracting logging of error and returning of None object, 101
 match structure for, 100
  handling specific value in a case object, 100
 Scala createCustomer method returning, 100
 using with CommandLine.options variable (example), 110
ORMs (object-relational models), lazy fetch, 76

P

parameter list, 7
passing a function to a function, 11
pattern matching, 2, 93–103
 converting if/else structure in Scala updateCustomerByIdList method, 96
 converting to pattern matches, 101

Scala, 66, 81

U

updateContactFor() method (example), using
    an immutable list, 53
updateContractForCustomerList() method (ex-
    ample), 52
updateCustomerByIdList() method (example),
    96–99

V

variables
    as placeholders in a specific scope, 49
    defining in Scala, 72
    immutable (see immutable variables)
    lazy, 67
    mutable, 43
    mutable, converting to immutable, 115
    strict evaluations and, 67
Visitor pattern, 112

volatile keyword, using with @Lazy annotation
    in Groovy, 72

W

web page for this book, xii

X

XXY company (example), 5
    (see also examples listed throughout)
    counting enabled customers with disabled
        contacts
        in single findAll(), 59
        iterative approach, 59
        recursive function, 60
        using function chaining, 59
    getting list of enabled contacts for enabled
        customers, 68
    refactoring countEnabledCustomersWith-
        NoEnabledContacts function, 62

About the Author

Joshua F. Backfield is a Senior Software Development Engineer at Dell SecureWorks, Inc., an industry-leading MSSP. He is responsible for the design and development of many internal UI tools, as well as multiple backend processes. He holds a bachelor of science in electronic systems technologies from Southern Illinois University at Carbondale, and a master's of science in computer science from DePaul University. He has worked in a variety of languages, such as C, C++, Perl, Java, JavaScript, and Scala, and he continues to learn and grow with more languages. He has ported multiple native C applications to Scala, introduced many coworkers to Scala, and taught them its underlying functional programming concepts.

Colophon

The animal on the cover of *Becoming Functional* is a sheldrake duck (*Tadorna tadorna*), also known as a common shelduck. The scientific name "tadorna" comes from the Celtic for "pied waterfowl" (which is also what shelduck means in 14th century English). The shelduck is widespread throughout Europe and Asia, near coastlines, lakes, rivers, salt marshes, and other water sources.

The word "pied" refers to having two or more different colors, and the sheldrake duck is indeed very colorful. It has a white body, a dark green head and neck, and both black and chestnut patches on the wings and chest. The beak is pinkish-orange, and in males, topped with a knob on the forehead. They are large ducks (closer to the size of a goose) that eat shellfish, aquatic snails, crustaceans, plant matter, and small fish.

During breeding season, shelducks build nests in tree hollows, dense bushes, rock clefts, or abandoned mammal burrows. Most shelduck populations migrate each summer to specific nesting sites. The largest of these is the Wadden Sea near Germany, where over 100,000 birds congregate each year.

Almost as soon as the young have hatched, their parents will depart for moulting grounds, leaving their offspring at a nearby "nursery" in the care of a few adults (usually those who did not breed themselves). These guardians watch over about 20 to 40 ducklings at a time, though the groupings change often. When the colony is approached, the adults give a warning call and fly into the air as decoys, while the young shelducks quickly dive underwater. By the fall, the ducklings are grown and able to migrate south.

The cover image is from Cassell's *Book of Birds*. The cover fonts are URW Typewriter and Guardian Sans. The text font is Adobe Minion Pro; the heading font is Adobe Myriad Condensed; and the code font is Dalton Maag's Ubuntu Mono.

Have it your way.

O'Reilly eBooks

- Lifetime access to the book when you buy through oreilly.com
- Provided in up to four, DRM-free file formats, for use on the devices of your choice: PDF, .epub, Kindle-compatible .mobi, and Android .apk
- Fully searchable, with copy-and-paste, and print functionality
- We also alert you when we've updated the files with corrections and additions.

oreilly.com/ebooks/

Safari Books Online

- Access the contents and quickly search over 7000 books on technology, business, and certification guides
- Learn from expert video tutorials, and explore thousands of hours of video on technology and design topics
- Download whole books or chapters in PDF format, at no extra cost, to print or read on the go
- Early access to books as they're being written
- Interact directly with authors of upcoming books
- Save up to 35% on O'Reilly print books

See the complete Safari Library at safari.oreilly.com

©2014 O'Reilly Media, Inc. O'Reilly logo is a registered trademark of O'Reilly Media, Inc. 14373

Get even more for your money.

Join the O'Reilly Community, and register the O'Reilly books you own. It's free, and you'll get:

- $4.99 ebook upgrade offer
- 40% upgrade offer on O'Reilly print books
- Membership discounts on books and events
- Free lifetime updates to ebooks and videos
- Multiple ebook formats, DRM FREE
- Participation in the O'Reilly community
- Newsletters
- Account management
- 100% Satisfaction Guarantee

Signing up is easy:

1. Go to: oreilly.com/go/register
2. Create an O'Reilly login.
3. Provide your address.
4. Register your books.

Note: English-language books only

To order books online:
oreilly.com/store

For questions about products or an order:
orders@oreilly.com

To sign up to get topic-specific email announcements and/or news about upcoming books, conferences, special offers, and new technologies:
elists@oreilly.com

For technical questions about book content:
booktech@oreilly.com

To submit new book proposals to our editors:
proposals@oreilly.com

O'Reilly books are available in multiple DRM-free ebook formats. For more information:
oreilly.com/ebooks

©2014 O'Reilly Media, Inc. O'Reilly logo is a registered trademark of O'Reilly Media, Inc. 14373

CPSIA information can be obtained at www.ICGtesting.com
Printed in the USA
LVOW03s1704170915

454592LV00029B/185/P

9 781449 368173